THE GLUTEN-FREE WAY

THE GLUTEN-FREE WAY
MY WAY

by

ADRIENNE Z. MILLIGAN

& WILLIAM MALTESE

THE BORGO PRESS

An Imprint of Wildside Press LLC

MMIX

Copyright © 2009 by Adrienne Z. Milligan and William Maltese
Cover by Deana C. Jamroz Copyright © 2009 by William Maltese.

All rights reserved.
No part of this book may be reproduced in any form
without the expressed written consent
of the authors and publisher.
Printed in the United States of America

www.wildsidepress.com

FIRST EDITION

CONTENTS

Disclaimer...9
Acknowledgments 10
Definitions 14

William Maltese #1: The Book Conceived 15
Preface 17
William Maltese #2: The Collaboration Begun 18
Chapter 1: My Introduction to the World of Gluten 20
Chapter 2: Being in the (Wheat) World, Not of the
    (Wheat) World...23
Chapter 3: Jonathan's Story 25
Chapter 4: Kelly's Story..29
Chapter 5: Difference in Pregnancies and Babies—With
    and Without Gluten 31
Chapter 6: Flourless Chocolate Torte............................32
Chapter 7: Going 100% Gluten-Free in the Home.........33
*William Maltese #3: Yes, 100% Gluten-Free, Doggone
    It!* 34
William Maltese #4: Reading, Writing, and GF 36
Chapter 8: Restraint: Avoiding the Poison....................39

Chapter 9: Medical Research and Staying Up-to-Date .. 41
Chapter 10: Go with Your Gut Instinct…Literally 43
Chapter 11: Traveling 44
William Maltese #5: Making It Easy on Uncle William 46
Chapter 12: Living with Someone Who Is GF When You're Not 48
William Maltese #6: 100% GF Isn't a Non-Stop Ticket to Paradise 50
Chapter 13: Cross-Contamination *IS* a Big Deal! 53
William Maltese #7: Recognizing the Signs 54
Chapter 14: Celiac Disease 56
Chapter 15: Cosmetics and Bath Products 57
Chapter 16: Medications and Vitamins 59
Chapter 17: Brain Fog: the Lack of Concentration and Focus 60
Chapter 18: My Challenges and Successes with the GF Way 62
Chapter 19: Eating Out the GF Way 65
William Maltese #8: The Long Wait 69
Chapter 20: Gluten-Free Baking Class: Home-Made Bread at Last! 71
Chapter 21: Creating My (Your) Own New Recipes 73
William Maltese #9: Good—A Matter of Taste 77
Chapter 22: Gluten-Free Eating Is a Lifestyle, Not a Diet 80
Chapter 23: What Do You Mean *That* Has Gluten in It? 82
William Maltese #10: Xoçai™ Chocolate 85
Chapter 24: My 100% Gluten-Free Way Idea of a Good Time 88
Chapter 25: Gluten-Free Gardening 90

Chapter 26: Gluten and Religious Observances..............91
Chapter 27: Other Do's and Don'ts................................92
William Maltese #11: One More Don't to Do 96

GLUTEN-FREE RECIPES

Note 98
Desserts..99
Cheese..116
Meat..123
Potatoes..132
Soup..134
Pasta Salad...136
Pancakes..137
Breads and Pie Dough...139

APPENDICES

Note 147
Appendix A: Celiac Disease Support Groups..............148
Appendix B: GF-Dedicated Companies That
   Make/Carry Only GF Products 150
Appendix C: Companies That Make GF Products.......153
Appendix D: Stores That Carry GF Products 157
Appendix E: Restaurants with GF Menus (or at the
   Least, GF Friendly) 159
Appendix F: Other GF Websites..................................162

Index of Recipes...163
About the Authors 166

Dedications

To Kelly Belly and Blue Eyes—

You have made my desire to live and research the Gluten-Free way a pleasure.
—Mama

and

To William and Olive—

Thank you for your love and support over the years. May you both rest in peace.

—The Authors

DISCLAIMER

This book is not intended to provide medical advice. Proper diagnosis of Celiac Sprue Disease or any other medical conditions needs to be sought from appropriate medical professionals. All contents of this book are the personal experiences and opinions of the authors.

All organizations, businesses, and product names mentioned in this book are the property of those individual organizations and businesses. In this day and age of the internet when so many organizations, businesses, and products are so often made mention of without their attending trademark designates ™ or ®, it's difficult to know when or if to provide these indicators. Even specific searches of U.S. Trademark Department files can often be confusing. So, more often than not, the authors have erred on the side of inclusion, rather than exclusion. If mistakes have been made, we shall make every attempt to make sure they're corrected in any subsequent editions of this book.

ACKNOWLEDGMENTS

To Carol Fenster—Thank you for sharing the story of your path to a GF lifestyle. It has made all the difference in providing an example for living healthy!

To Cutestuff—Thank you for having an open mind and choosing the Gluten-Free lifestyle to good health. Thanks, too, for being a guinea pig for our GF Way of baking.

To Elaine—Thank you for insisting that Jonathan "get off of the wheat," and for your encouragement over the years as we've learned about the GF lifestyle, foods, and research.

To friends and family—Thank you for your honesty about the various recipes to which we've subjected you over the years.

To FlyLady—Thank you for teaching that anything can be accomplished in fifteen minutes! (Yes, even a few pages of this book.)

To Chris Baty—Thank you for your book and NaNoWriMo. Though our book wasn't written during November, your advice, suggestions, and example on how to write a book were invaluable to Adrienne.

To the Companies and Restaurants that make and/or carry GF Foods—All who live the GF lifestyle are grateful to those of you who create, sell, carry, and provide GF items in stores, bakeries, and restaurants. Thank you for making items safe for the gluten-intolerant to consume.

To Jennigizerbunny—Thank you for taking the time to create a GF pie crust recipe for us to use and for making sure there's always GF food in your home for Adrienne's two boys.

More Acknowledgments

To The Fearless Bread Chef—Your GF baking class at Marlene's Market & Deli® in Federal Way, WA, was a joy to watch. Thank you for your GF bread recipe that's yummy, quick, and easy to make!

To Torte Man—Thank you for the scrumptious chocolate torte and baking advice!

To N7NAP and Diane—Thanks for helping tweak GF recipes for Dutch oven cooking. It's an honor to have been a part of your family's path to the GF lifestyle.

To RJS—You hold in your hand Adrienne's first published book. Now it's *your* turn to publish!

To Security 1—Thank you for helping Adrienne to face a fear by soaring her to new heights. May the winds always blow in your "Miss Direction."

To DC132—Thank you for being there and encouraging Adrienne to follow her dreams. She now knows she's "Somebody" even when "It's No Good."

To Bluejay—Thank you for always being there when needed.

To "T"—Lemon Bars (GF, of course) are waiting for you. Just give an hour advance notice.

To Bullwinkle, SiteImpressions, Firefighter Joe, Chatterbug, MaxwellMama, Raymond & Debra—Thank you for always being there!

To Zebra Pen—Adrienne truly appreciates your fine products (specifically the F-402) as this is what she used to write the majority of her part of this book. (http://www.zebrapen.com/)

To Janis at WW—Thank you for being an amazing example; just so you know, Adrienne is with you "till she dies."

To Sweet Beauty OrganicChocolate Spa® Treatments—Your Taste Lip Balm made the writing process more enjoyable by providing that always amazing aroma of chocolate.

To Pandora—Thank you for proofing and asking the questions to help make this happen.

To My Muse—Thank you for encouraging me to just "be."

To Wildside/Borgo Press—Thank you for helping us make this non-gluten book a reality.

To My Uncle Bill—Without you, this book would not have been published in 2009 (or possibly ever). Adrienne.

To My Niece Adrienne—Without you, this book would not have been published in 2009 (or possibly ever). William.

To Bonnie Clark, the "Empress of Xoçai™ Chocolate" who I hope will be inspired by this to write that book on grill cooking for small-boat owners.

To Our Heavenly Father and Savior—Our eternal gratitude for the gift to write, the passion to write often, and the inspiration that kept the words flowing.

DEFINITIONS

GLUTEN—A mixture of plant proteins occurring in cereal grains—chiefly wheat…(kamut, spelt), barley (including barley malt), rye, and triticale…and oats due to cross-contamination of farming and harvesting practices—to which many people are allergic.

GLUTEN-FREE WAY—A way of life recommended to combat the negative aspects of Celiac Disease and wheat allergies; it excludes all gluten-containing elements—like wheat…(kamut, spelt), barley (including barley malt), rye, and triticale…and oats due to cross-contamination of farming and harvesting practices.

WILLIAM MALTESE MOMENT #1

THE BOOK CONCEIVED

This book is primarily written from the first-person perspective of my niece, Adrienne Z. Milligan, because it's mainly the ongoing story of her concentrated efforts to find the cause of, and instigate the elimination of, the initially mysterious source of health problems that were visited upon her family.

For many years, I existed on the sidelines, merely watching and being impressed by her efforts to cope, discover the culprit (gluten), and convert her family into living a completely Gluten-Free Way. In the end, of course, as a long-time published author, I couldn't help but recognize the obvious value her experiences might have for others who face similar health problems and seemingly insurmountable dietary roadblocks, sometimes without even a clue. With that incentive in mind, I approached my niece about the possibility for this collaborative effort.

Along the way, I have, of course, added my constant input, by way of hopefully stimulating, improving, and supplementing my co-author's narrative. Quite by way of marvelous side effect, I've seen my own health benefit tremendously from my participation and experimentation in the formulation, collection, and tasting of GF-Way information and recipes for this book.

PREFACE

When I was approached about writing this book, I was afraid I wouldn't have enough to say to fill its pages. However, more than one person said that I "could talk for hours on GF living and never repeat" myself. So, here goes!

—Adrienne Z. Milligan

WILLIAM MALTESE MOMENT #2

THE COLLABORATION BEGUN

A lot of people seem to think that all they need is a good idea, and from that they can easily write a book. Take it from someone who has written and had published over 200 books—me—writing even one book, even with a good idea upon which to base it, isn't easy; it takes a lot of time, effort, and keep-at-it concentration.

Nor does a collaborative effort necessarily make the book-writing process any easier; remember the old saying about the possible problems of more than one cook in any kitchen.

While I consider myself extremely lucky to have recognized my niece and her family's story as one well worth relating, I have to admit that its conversion into book form wasn't nearly as easily managed as I originally envisioned. Primarily, I blame myself for having been so long in the writing business that I forgot some of the trials, tribulations, anxiety, doubt, tedium, and pressure of a deadline that can obsess someone new to writing, my niece included. In the end, though, which is so important, Adrienne did finally manage to pull her wits and writing skills together sufficiently to do her part in bringing this volume to fruition.

CHAPTER ONE

MY INTRODUCTION TO THE WORLD OF GLUTEN

Until 2001, I had never heard the term "gluten." I had no idea that Celiac Disease was an auto-immune disorder. I did not know that gluten was a protein found in wheat, rye, and barley. "Cross-contamination" in regards to farming, harvesting, and food-preparation practices was completely unknown to me.

The Gluten-Free Way was a whole new concept to me when I first Googled "wheat free recipes" in June of 2001 because my mother-in-law was coming for a visit, had a wheat allergy, and I wanted to make sure that the food I fixed for her was food she could eat without getting sick. My on-line search popped up a long list of wheat-free recipes along with supplementary hits for "Celiac Sprue," "Celiac Disease," and "Gluten Intolerance." I read with interest how Carol Fenster (a Gluten-Free cookbook author) discovered that she had Celiac Disease and was gluten-intolerant.

Carol explained her life before going Gluten-Free. I read her story and saw many things identical to my husband Jonathan's health, behavior, and complaints about how he always felt. Suddenly, I was anxious for Jonathan to get home from work to let him know that I'd possibly found the long sought-after answer as to why he always felt so crummy.

When he came home, he was, as usual, as General Manager of our local pizzeria, covered in wheat-flour dust. I told him I wanted to read him something and asked him to keep an open mind. He agreed, and I proceeded to read him Carol's story. During which, Jonathan kept interrupting with comments like, "That's me, as well as Carol, when growing up."—"That's how I feel even now!"—"That's definitely me."

After I was done reading, Jonathan read Carol's story, yet again, just so he could more fully take it in and ponder its implications.

From that day forward, Jonathan and I have done our level best to keep him 100% Gluten-Free. Admittedly, he does still get "glutened" on occasion—not by choice but usually by cross-contamination, or via unclear labels on foods, but when asked if he'd ever go back to gluten, his response is always the same, "You couldn't *pay* me enough to go back!"

My family went Gluten-Free in 2001, before we really understood the full health benefits that would result from our doing so, and before Jonathan was officially tested to verify that, yes, he did have Celiac Disease. We're still Gluten-Free and tremendously happy to be so.

This book, then, is a glimpse into our family and life since stepping onto the Gluten-Free Way. There have been obstacles along the way, to be sure, but nothing so challenging that we haven't been able to maneuver around them.

Neither my husband nor I will admit to it being an easy way to go, over these past years, but we're convinced it has improved not only the quality of our lives, but the lives of our two children.

My early, and admittedly difficult, days of wondering what and how to buy or fix Gluten-Free meals for my family are pretty much over and done. Those of you now starting out on the Gluten-Free Way have a far easier time of it, with far larger selections of GF-Way food stuffs, than I did. More and more companies have started to provide yummy non-gluten entrees and deserts as it becomes more and more apparent that Celiac Disease is more wide spread than anyone originally thought.

Just a couple weeks ago, I saw an ad in a local store's health newsletter that Glutenfreeda™ is now even making GF instant-oatmeal packets and GF burritos—both unavailable when my family began our non-gluten journey.

CHAPTER TWO

BEING IN THE (WHEAT) WORLD, NOT OF THE (WHEAT) WORLD

When people learn of the gluten intolerance and wheat allergy that Jonathan and my boys have, one of their most frequent questions is, "How can anyone *possibly* live without wheat?" Okay, so it wasn't so easy back in 2001—that was super-tough going. It was even more difficult to exclude all gluten which is found not only in wheat, rye, and barley, but in non-certified GF oats as well.

However, a large amount of Gluten-Free products suddenly popping up all over the place has made it a lot easier.

Most people can learn to accept Gluten-Free versions of their beloved wheat/gluten food stuffs and can learn all of the literally thousands of products that contain gluten and need to be avoided.

In addition to learning how to accept the Gluten-Free versions of their favorite goods, the Gluten-Free Way requires a definite change of mind-set. For those of you who have been diagnosed Celiac/gluten-sensitive, you must be 100% Gluten-Free to be 100% healthy. The Gluten-Free

Way isn't a road you travel just sometimes or occasionally, but all day every day.

Once you get the mind-set that the Gluten-Free Way is FOR LIFE, and that you will emerge healthier because of it, it does get easier!

Over time, a lot of you will lose your cravings for certain gluten foods that you thought you'd never be able to live without. I think a lot of it has to do with you becoming healthier, and your body realizing all the advantages in jettisoning cravings that only make you sick. There are still items that Jonathan misses, but the benefits of his being Gluten-Free outweigh the horrible reactions he has to gluten (especially gluten mixed with dairy—yikes!).

CHAPTER THREE

JONATHAN'S STORY

My wife, Adrienne, asked me to put down my memories of how my family self-diagnosed our problems with wheat and what we did to deal with them.

It started when I was just beginning the third or fourth grade. For some time, my father thought I had an allergy to wheat and my mother thought he was simply crazy. My parents started me on a regiment of Sudafed® to control the coughing fits that I was experiencing. I was also experiencing uncontrollable headaches, mood swings, inability to concentrate, difficulty in school, etc. One Saturday for some reason I didn't have anything with wheat in it all day. For dinner, my mother made whole wheat pancakes. My father made the offhand comment, "What do you want to bet he'll be coughing his head off in a couple of minutes?" Within a few minutes, I was clearing my throat. The next day, a simple change in diet made my headache and cough go away. This began a journey of self-diagnosis, and guessing by my mother, to find out what was wrong with the family.

The first thing that we did was to stop feeding me anything with wheat in it. We didn't understand until almost twenty years later that the culprit was truly gluten. The changes we did make were to replace everything I ate that contained wheat with either corn- or rye-based foods. I remember my peanut-butter-and-jelly sandwiches where made on hard rye crackers. We later replaced these with a wheat-free rye bread that was much more palatable. This diet change helped with the coughing and the headaches to some extent but still didn't remedy them.

I had a difficult time with my brother and was always physically fighting with him. One hot sticky summer night, while I was on the top bed of our bunk beds, my brother would not stop clearing his throat. I remember not being able to control my anger and just losing control. I climbed down off of the top bunk and punched him in the stomach, then climbed back into my bunk to wait for my parents to come and discipline me. This typifies the uncontrollable mood swings that came over me when I ate gluten.

A year after going off wheat, we switched to goat's milk and started to avoid things made with cow's milk, because of the stomach pains and issues that my brother and I were having. These stomach issues continued for years. My brother and I had gastrointestinal-tract tests done that required us to drink barium and water and then have X-rays taken to try and find out what was wrong with us; of course, they didn't reveal anything. Finally, we were told that we were lactose intolerant and to avoid milk products. This was about the time I was in seventh grade.

During High School, I would self-regulate my wheat intake based on how I wanted to handle the symptoms of my "allergy" and its associated problems. If I knew a party was coming up, or a camp-out, I could base how I'd feel by how much wheat I ate. Also during high school, my mother was diagnosed with irritable-bowel syndrome.

At some time in my early twenties, I heard somewhere that my problem was most likely related to the protein in wheat, rye, and barley which is gluten. I started to realize that even the rye I was eating would cause the headaches and the mood swings; I just needed to eat it in larger quantities than wheat for it to affect me. I decided that I would stop messing with the rye and "manage" my wheat intake. I got to the point where I could identify in less than five minutes if I had anything with wheat in it. My best friend called me a hypochondriac because I was always complaining of not feeling well. I was easily depressed. My stomach problems kept me from ever thinking of drinking milk, and I rarely ate cheese or ice cream. I would have the stomach cramps even if I didn't have milk products, and I would think I must have had milk somewhere. I also recall that I referred to wheat as "my addiction." I would get a "high" off of eating it, and would have to continue to eat it to continue the high. When I would stop eating it, I would go through withdrawal symptoms of sorts. The cravings were intense and sometimes uncontrollable and, once I started eating it, again, I would eat it for days on end until I would feel so horrible that I would (eventually) have to stop.

How grateful I am that all of that has changed since my family embarked upon the 100% Gluten-Free Way, especially since having come to realize that my problem is gluten, not lactose, allows me to drink milk, eat ice cream, and enjoy cheese, without fearing any of them (as long as they're GF) as I once did.

CHAPTER FOUR

KELLY'S STORY

When our first son, Kelly, was born, Jonathan and I thought for sure his constant screaming after eating was a sign of chronic colic. Let me rephrase that: *Everyone* around Kelly for any length of time told us, "He has colic!" Since I believed that after the first three to six months, colic should no longer be a major issue for any baby, I became convinced it had to be something else, but I didn't have a clue as to what.

Jonathan would, literally, walk Kelly all around the house every night and, sometimes, even during the day, to help my son fall asleep. Jonathan and I didn't get much sleep, either, the first year and a half of Kelly's life. Our son was always screaming, crying; his pain was always pitiful and obvious, at such times, in his eyes and on his face.

Until finding out about Celiac Disease, I didn't connect the dots that put Kelly's eating of gluten as the real cause of his screaming, crying, and hurting.

Only after I read about Celiac Disease did I notice how twenty minutes after Kelly ate something with gluten in it he would begin screaming and his tears would start to flow—as regular as clockwork.

I'd feed Kelly a bowl of cereal that had barley in it, and twenty minutes later on the dot (I timed it), he started crying and screaming. I fed him Gerber® Baby Rice Cereal (Gluten-Free), and nothing happened. That was enough for both Jonathan and me to say, "No more gluten for Kelly!"

Something else that we didn't know until after it was too late to do anything about it (at least as far as Kelly was concerned), is that gluten is passed through breast milk. I ate a lot of gluten while pregnant with and while nursing Kelly, having had no idea that the gluten in my breast milk was what made him suffer so much pain twenty minutes after EACH AND EVERY time I nursed him.

CHAPTER FIVE

DIFFERENCES IN PREGNANCIES AND BABIES— WITH AND WITHOUT GLUTEN

During my first pregnancy, and while breastfeeding my first born, I ate wheat and gluten—lots of it.

During my second pregnancy, and while breastfeeding my second child, I ate strictly according to the GF Way. There was all the difference in the world. Ozias' disposition was decidedly more low-key, less hyper, and less painful than the gluten-plagued overloads experienced by his older brother.

CHAPTER SIX

FLOURLESS CHOCOLATE TORTE

A friend of ours, whom I respectfully dubbed "Torte Man," went to culinary arts school to become a baker. He and I often discussed my family's GF-Way regimen; so, one day, he brought over a flourless chocolate torte made with only butter, eggs, sugar, and cream. WOW! Talk about delicious! It was rich and naturally Gluten-Free.

When Jonathan and I had our tenth wedding anniversary, Torte Man was kind enough again to make his wonderful chocolate torte. We again enjoyed every rich GF chocolate bite of it. When we shared some of it with friends, they were amazed that something so delicious could be Gluten-Free.

Every time I see Torte Man (which is fairly often), I smile, because he helped me see just how good GF food can be, and that it doesn't have to be taste-free and/or disgusting.

(See the Recipe section for Flourless Chocolate Torte.)

CHAPTER SEVEN

GOING 100% GLUTEN-FREE IN THE HOME

For awhile, after discovering Jonathan and Kelly's gluten problems, I cooked two of everything: one Gluten-Free for them, one not necessarily GF for me. Then, I decided enough duplication was enough. I committed even myself to the Gluten-Free Way of life and gave away to friends all of our gluten-containing food, our gluten-contaminated plates, pots, pans, and eating utensils, replacing one and all to provide us with a 100% GF-Way environment. My family and I have tremendously benefited health-wise from that very wise decision.

WILLIAM MALTESE MOMENT #3

YES, 100% GLUTEN-FREE, DOGGONE IT!

I've an acquaintance in the writing world, Bo Perkins, writer and editor, who was told by her doctors to go on a wheat-free, Gluten-Free diet because of her allergies. She simply ignored them.

Awhile back, though, she adopted a nine-year-old yellow Labrador dog who went into a choking fit that the vet diagnosed as—can you guess?—the result of allergies. The vet's suggested treatment for the dog—can you guess?—a wheat-free, Gluten-Free diet.

Since the dog had so wormed his way into Bo's heart that she couldn't possibly do anything else but try to make his life easier, she started cooking him wheat-free and Gluten-Free food and weaning him off commercial dog foods (the latter laden with wheat and gluten). After four months, the dog was thirty-five pounds lighter and acting like a young pup—able to run farther, faster; able to learn better, faster—without nearly as many accompanying sneezes, wheezes and coughs.

Along with the dog's improvement, Bo's health took a marked turn toward the better, as a direct result of her having shared the wheat-free, Gluten-Free food she'd prepared for him. She has fewer allergy attacks and has had zero asthma attacks since her dog and she have—doggone it!—joined the GF Way.

WILLIAM MALTESE MOMENT #4

READING, WRITING, AND GF

While maintaining a Gluten-Free environment on the home front is one thing, it isn't going to happen at school where most children spend even more time than they do at home.

While my niece and her husband have solved that problem by home-schooling all of their children, not all parents can go that route, or choose to do so, making it extremely important that gluten-intolerant children are pre-prepared for spending so much of their lives in surroundings abounding with something that can be so potentially dangerous to them.

It's genuinely difficult for a child not to want to partake of the same foods and snacks, from school vending machines and from school lunch rooms, which are eaten by fellow classmates. It's very difficult for a gluten-intolerant child to face down the stares and curious glances when someone's mother sends freshly baked cookies and the gluten-intolerant kid is the only one in the classroom who doesn't partake.

Who hasn't read accounts of truly malicious children who know full well the dietary restrictions of their fellows and take full advantage? While the stories that usually make the newspapers are accounts of kids with peanut allergies having fatal reactions to being purposely slipped tainted foodstuff, I've had more than one parent tell me that the same sort of mischievousness has been played out between gluten-intolerant children and some unscrupulous classmates. Unfortunately, the gluten-related incidents can be perceived by authoritative figures as far less serious than the peanut-related ones in that the short-term results of the former don't see the victimized child dropping dead on the spot.

It's up to every parent to make sure his gluten-intolerant child is equipped with all of the knowledge needed in order for that child to cope at school; including daily brown-bagging of the proper Gluten-Free foods for school lunches to keep temptation for gluten-laden substitutes at a minimum.

Teachers and classmates should be made aware of any gluten-intolerant child among them so as better to monitor situations, in the absence of parents, and/or to recognize gluten-allergy reactions when they occur. While some parents have the tendency to listen to the pleadings of their child to not do anything that sets him apart as "being different" from his peers, a child should be reassured that he'll come across as decidedly less different if his condition is explained and understood. Thinking little gluten-intolerant Charlie is suddenly a bully and uncaring terror is less preferable than recognizing his body is merely reacting to gluten-poisoning.

Even later in life, with years of indoctrination and trial and error which should provide anyone the firm basis on which to resist temptation, there are always pitfalls with which to deal. Fraternity and sorority venues often include keg parties; yes, beer, more often than not, contains gluten. Such get-togethers can provide all sorts of grain-based gluten-filled alcoholic beverages, too. Peer pressure, and a desire to "fit in," can constantly make it genuinely difficult, if not impossible, for a gluten-intolerant anyone—man, woman, or child—to resist being "one of the group" by indulging in just one gluten-saturated beer, cocktail, Ding Dong®, or cookie.

No matter how well-intentioned and determined any one, or any one family, is to be 100% Gluten-Free 100% of the time, it's simply not going to happen, as my niece and any member of her family can tell you. You can only do your very best to educate yourself and your gluten-intolerant loved ones on the subject to provide all the reassurances necessary to bolster die-hard determination to stay on the Gluten-Free Way. When any of you slip, inadvertently or with full knowledge, you simply have to recognize the resulting consequences to your well-being as the result of your misstep, and do your best to get back on the straight and narrow as quickly as possible.

No one is perfect; nor should anyone, not even you, expect you to be.

CHAPTER EIGHT

RESTRAINT: AVOIDING THE POISON

"What is food to one, is to others bitter poison."
—Lucretius (96 BC – 55 BC),
De Rerum Natura

Avoiding gluten is not always easy. We would never pretend that it is.

There are constant temptations to cheat. There are countless items that most of us, including us authors, are shocked to learn contain gluten.

Gluten is in almost every aspect of life: from food, to office, to daycare....

Here's a list of possibly gluten-contaminated things you might want to avoid:

For those who love BBQ sauces, be on the lookout for BBQ sauces made with beer, unless it's GF beer. Yes, GF beer is made in the U.S. and Canada by several breweries. Regular beer is made from wheat, barley, or rye. So are a lot of liquors that should, likewise, be avoided.

Vanilla extract is usually made with grain alcohol. Does the gluten remain after the vanilla is distilled? Is the grain alcohol safe? Same question should be asked about vinegar.

Imitation crab is nine times out of ten made with wheat flour.

Some cheeses have gluten fillers.

Some lunch meats have fillers or injections of gluten-rich broth.

Delis, buffets, and potlucks can provide lots of chances for cross-contamination as utensils are switched quickly between different foods and dishes. One minute, a serving spoon is in GF potatoes; next minute, it's deep in gluten-saturated macaroni.

Bakeries and pizza parlors have wheat-flour dust that can remain in the air for twenty-four hours or more.

Glue on envelopes can have gluten. So can the adhesive on stickers and postage stamps.

Play dough is more often than not made with wheat flour.

Dentists give out toothpastes that may contain gluten—be sure to ask.

Some medications use gluten as a binding agent or filler.

Some candy is dusted with wheat flour to keep it from sticking when packaged.

Some seasonings contain wheat flour/gluten to help eliminate clumping.

Some cosmetics, lotions, creams contain wheat/flour gluten, too—be sure to check their labels.

CHAPTER NINE

MEDICAL RESEARCH AND STAYING UP-TO-DATE

Do what we do:

Sign up on a GF email group as many members are likely even more on top of things than you are.

Type in various search words into Google®, Swagbucks®, or your favorite search engine for more information. Try using search words such as: Celiac Disease, Celiac Sprue, gluten-allergy, Gluten-Free, gluten intolerance, wheat allergy, gluten sensitivity, rye, barley, oats, wheat, and spelt. Search out, as well, doctors and clinics that specialize in CELIAC DISEASE research.

Go to the Mayo Clinic® website at:

www.mayoclinic.com

and read what they have on CELIAC DISEASE.

Read up on the University of Maryland's Celiac Disease Research Center and what they're studying.

Check out books from the library.

Buy those books that you want to have immediately at hand for reference other than just for the length available during a book's library check-out time.

Create a wish list on Amazon.com for GF books and for GF foods that you'd like to have; so others know what foods they can get for you.

Search out support groups and classes that may have more information.

Read our blog and visit our web-sites:

http://www.theglutenfreewaymyway.com

and

http://www.facebook.com/group.php?gid=91859902695&ref=mf

CHAPTER TEN

GO WITH YOUR GUT INSTINCT…LITERALLY

We cannot emphasize enough —
If you feel that something doesn't look right, or may have gluten in it (*no matter what someone else tells you*), **DON'T BUY OR EAT IT!**

CHAPTER ELEVEN

TRAVELING

Making the most of a vacation while living the GF Way is easier if you follow some of these tips:

1. Plan ahead—check your favorite national chains (such as Whole Foods Markets®) to see if they have a store near or at your destination. The best way to enjoy your vacation is to be healthy and take the GF Way the entire time. The worst way to vacation is to end up gluten contaminated even if you're told a food is GF; allergic-reactions times get faster and are worse the longer you're GF.
2. Take as much GF-Way foodstuffs and personal care items as you can with you. If you're flying and/or going international, be sure to check the requirements and regulations of airlines, customs, cruises, ships, *et cetera*, to keep up-to-date. If you have an official diagnosis from your doctor, you may be able to take more items with you than someone who doesn't—again, check with the companies you are using for your travel.

3. There is at least one GF-travel group, Bob and Ruth's Gluten-Free Dining and Travel Club®, that regularly takes cruises and field trips. When on a cruise ship, this group provides a dedicated GF kitchen so that those who are eating don't have to worry about cross-contamination. How cool is that?
4. Some places, like certain time-share condos, have special services that allow you to pay and provide a grocery list to the staff before you arrive. The staff will purchase and place your items in your condo for you. I've had the option to do this, but have yet to try it, mainly because we've always gone to a condo close enough that we can take most of our own GF food with us and/or find it in destination stores with regular stocks of GF food.

WILLIAM MALTESE MOMENT #5

MAKING IT EASY ON UNCLE WILLIAM

Over the years, my niece and her family have visited me on many occasions. Since they live across state, their every visit usually is accompanied by a few-days' stay. During which times, they are transferred from the safe GF environment of their home to the more danger-laden often gluten-glutted environment of their Uncle William's home; I'm neither gluten intolerant nor allergic to wheat.

Such visits could be difficult for both my niece and her family and for me without the preplanning that, instead, makes them pure pleasantries instead of dreaded inconveniences.

Days before such happenings, there's frequent communication between us wherein decisions are made as to what every meal will be once they get here, what they'll bring with them, and what I'll need to have on hand. Usually their packing includes the majority of all the GF foodstuffs they'll need for the extent of their stay—snacks for themselves and the kids, pasta, bread, flour, any pre-mixed desserts they might want to eat while they're here.... Of course, they're by now familiar enough with the stores selling GF products in my neighborhood in case they need anything.

Once here, Jonathan and Adrienne, more often than not, jump in and assist in the food preparation, partially out of their good-graciousness, but partly, I'm sure, to insure their own health. There's always at least one meal of Jonathan's GF lasagna (See Recipe at end of book) that I like so much that I've made it a "must" for their every visit, and a selection of several GF desserts. Since Jonathan is, also, far better at barbecuing than I am, he invariably volunteers for that as well.

By just such careful collaboration, consultation, and cooperation…by allowing them full access to my kitchen and full participation in the choices and, often, in the preparation of what I have on hand to feed them…their visits come off without a hitch. In fact, we have everything so much down to a science these days that any problems, if any, usually arise outside my home, as when we visited the supposedly GF bakery and Jonathan and the kids suffered the effects of gluten cross-contamination that occurred there.

CHAPTER TWELVE

LIVING WITH SOMEONE WHO IS GF WHEN YOU'RE NOT

There are two ways to live with someone who needs to be GF when you're not.

Have two of everything and worry about cross-contamination *every time* food is prepared.

Or….

Make life easier and safer for your family member(s) who must live GF by taking the GF road yourself and providing them with a 100% GF-home environment.

Yes, going 100% GF does take a bit of adjusting, and I speak from personal experience. Yes, there are foods that you will miss but, believe me, you can deal with it.

Your loved ones who need to live GF in order to feel well will thank you for their not feeling lousy, being sick, having reactions, or spending more time under the weather than out in it enjoying life in general.

Life does change when a household goes GF—or even when one person goes GF. It doesn't have to be a bad thing, though, unless you allow it to be. There are days when eating GF will seem like such a chore, but it's all in how the participants look at the GF Way and come to know, accept, and desire the true benefits to be had from adhering to it. My family and I have *always* found the pluses far outweigh any minuses.

As my boys have gotten older, I've involved them more and more in helping select food in stores, in order to give them a better sense of having some control over what they eat.

My oldest has been reading labels for years and now reads them all the time. My younger already recognizes "Gluten-Free" as printed on boxes, packages, cans, and containers.

Often, I try to make shopping fun for them by asking them to point out all of the GF products they can. Occasionally, I even provide a GF-candy bar by way of reward to whomever finds a GF product first.

WILLIAM MALTESE MOMENT #6

100% GF Isn't a Non-Stop Ticket to Paradise

So, you're irritable, feeling bum, grumpy, and flushed, likewise with a headache and attending body aches and pains…or your other half, and/or kids are irritable, feeling bum, grumpy, and flushed, likewise with a headache, attending body aches and pains….

So, you all head off on the Gluten-Free Way, and suddenly you're all less irritable, feeling less bum, grumpy, flushed, likewise with fewer headaches and attending body aches and pains….

Just don't assume that the 100% Gluten-Free Way is going to see you 100% of the time 100% free of irritability, feeling less bum, grumpy, and flushed, likewise with no more headaches and/or attending body aches and pains, because it just isn't going to happen, if just because those symptoms aren't exclusively the result of wheat- or gluten allergies. They can be caused, and will continue to be caused, by a whole gamut of contributing factors, including simple human nature, stress, and fatigue.

When you're overly tired or stressed out, you'll still get irritable, nothing to do with wheat or gluten. When someone doesn't do what you want them to do, or what you think they should do, you'll still get grumpy, nothing to do with wheat or gluten. If you have the flu, you'll still feel bum, likely have a temperature and feel flushed, and will still have all of the attending body aches and pains common to every flu sufferer, nothing to do with wheat or gluten.

I have had moments when I've found my niece and her husband's children, 100% Gluten-Free as they may be, just as obnoxious as their wheat- and gluten-saturated peers. I have had moments when I've found my niece, who in no way suffers from wheat- and/or gluten-allergies, and who benefits in so many favorable ways from her adoption of the Gluten-Free Way, far more irritable than her gluten-intolerant husband, even when he's inadvertently come off the Gluten-Free Way because of cross-contamination. Human nature can make you mean and spiteful, say things you wish later that you hadn't said or do things that you later wish that you hadn't done. If being 100% Gluten-Free can make all of the above less frequent, maybe even less intense, just don't think that it gives you a free pass to some kind of earth-bound paradise wherein all will be right in your world 24/7.

The Gluten-Free Way is not a be-all cure-all way of living. That said, it can—especially for those of you with wheat or gluten allergies—make your life better, healthier, and let you live longer. Take those blessings it does provide, embrace them, make them yours, and see them merely as the tools they are that better equip you to deal with life's many other obstacles and pitfalls that have nothing whatsoever to do with your negative responses to wheat and/or to some protein molecules found within it.

CHAPTER THIRTEEN

CROSS-CONTAMINATION *IS* A BIG DEAL!

Cross-contamination is a HUGE issue for anyone with allergies or intolerances.

Cross-contamination can occur anywhere there is gluten and non-gluten food or products in the same facility, home, school, workplace, environment.... It can happen while you're eating out, eating in a friend's kitchen, buying food from bulk bins, grabbing a bag of GF flour in contact with a bag of wheat flour.... The list goes on and on.

One thing that we have found to help flush out gluten fairly fast is drinking a lot of lemon water as close to 100% lemon juice as possible. My boys can handle a lot of "pucker power," so they ingest more lemon juice than Jonathan can. The more they drink, the faster the toxins (the gluten) seem to get flushed out of their systems.

WILLIAM MALTESE MOMENT #7

RECOGNIZING THE SIGNS

Adrienne and her whole family met up with me in Spokane for Adrienne and I to discuss the progress of this book, and we all decided to visit a local bakery. Hardly a city known for its innovations, Spokane, Washington, is a rather laid-back, conservative, and little-changing town, and I was frankly pretty amazed to find it with a bakery suddenly advertising products catering to GF consumers. Certainly, Adrienne and I thought it warranted a visit and a recommendation, if possible, from us to you.

The bakery staff was friendly and charming. The GF selection of bakery goods was numerous and tasty. All in all, we were genuinely pleased with what we saw, what we heard, what we ate.

Well-pleased and satisfied, we left the establishment and started off for our next stop—my cousin's house; my cousin is convinced that Xoçai™ chocolates are an ideal complement to anyone's GF lifestyle (more about that, later).

Within minutes of leaving the bakery, Jonathan was obviously in distress. He was fidgety. He was sweaty. His face was flushed. He recognized his symptoms and asked for an allergy pill and aspirin to alleviate at least some of his discomfort. The meds helped.

Adrienne monitored their two boys, closely, as we proceeded to our pre-scheduled appointment to sample Xoçai™ chocolate.

While my co-author, and I ate chocolate at my cousin's, Adrienne's sons played with my cousin's two dogs. What initially came across as merely the rambunctiousness of two ordinary children enjoying fun and games with willing animals, soon escalated to an entirely different level that we all recognized as anything but ordinary.

Adrienne and Jonathan were quick with allergy medicine that slowed the kids down but didn't entirely solve the problem. Kelly and Ozias remained hyper long after we got them back to my place, and Jonathan had passed out in the bedroom. All this was the result of one bakery having mixed and/or baked its GF products in the same environment in which it baked its gluten products.

CHAPTER FOURTEEN

CELIAC DISEASE

GLUTEN SHOULD BE SEEN AS DEADLY FOR THOSE WITH CELIAC DISEASE!

CHAPTER FIFTEEN

COSMETICS AND BATH PRODUCTS

Shampoos and makeup, along with lotions and potions, often contain gluten. The official verdict is still out on whether or not these items, used externally, affect anyone with CELIAC DISEASE. Jonathan, though, can't use any shampoo that has gluten in it. His head starts to itch to the point where, the first time, we initially mistook the symptoms for head lice. Once I figured out the real cause, by reading the label and seeing the shampoo contained wheat, Jonathan stopped using it, and his itching went away.

Since our home is 100% GF, we choose not to buy any products with any gluten content. We'd rather be safe than sorry.

Makeup isn't easy for me to get without gluten which manufacturers have long found is an excellent binding agent. So, gluten-intolerant ladies, beware!

Even items that one wouldn't normally think as having gluten very well may. So always be on the alert. For instance, my boys wore Breathe Right® Nasal Strips, and their noses broke out in a rash. I checked the product's website which said only that the product used "medical-grade adhesive." I've emailed for more specifics but have yet to receive a reply.

CHAPTER SIXTEEN

MEDICATIONS AND VITAMINS

Make sure that all of your medical records and pharmacy records indicate which members of your family are "allergic" to gluten, because you'll want to avoid gluten in your vitamins and prescribed medications. Of course, if it's ever a question of either taking a gluten-laced medicine or having you or a loved one die, that's a decision to be made, at the time, on an individual basis. There are, though, many alternative medications that don't have gluten, and those are the ones you should always try to buy. Some local pharmacists can, if asked, actually even duplicate some medications in-house, using fillers and binders, such as xanthan gum or corn starch, other than gluten.

CHAPTER SEVENTEEN

BRAIN FOG: THE LACK OF CONCENTRATION AND FOCUS

Some people have a difficult time converting to a GF Way, because their ingestion of gluten doesn't always warrant immediate trips to the emergency room. Their reaction to gluten isn't the same obviously dire reactions of people with allergies to peanut butter or to bee venom; either of the last two can all-too-quickly be life-threatening on each and every occasion.

Ingesting gluten is a more subtle killer, life-threatening over the long run. A gluten-intolerant person's body undergoes slow internal damage, headaches, and brain fog. The latter is especially dangerous if a person is driving, operating heavy machinery, or doing anything that would be hazardous without clear thinking.

Jonathan and I are acutely aware of the dangers of possible impending brain fog. Whenever he senses it anywhere in the offing, he immediately stops the car and turns the driving over to me.

There have been times when I've had to drive home because Jonathan has been too foggy-headed to figure out where the car was parked, and/or he had such a pounding gluten-related headache that he was too debilitated to drive.

The immediate response to ingesting gluten isn't the same for each person. Fortunately, my boys and Jonathan seem to have many of the same responses, when they are simultaneously glutened, if with different response times. It's not ideal, but it usually does make it easier for us to pinpoint what's going on—whether from something eaten, or touched.

CHAPTER EIGHTEEN

MY CHALLENGES AND SUCCESSES WITH THE GF WAY

I try not to use soy, since it can be a big allergen, plus I personally don't like its aftertaste. Nor do I use any bean flours, like fava and garbafava. I try to limit my use of corn flour, as some people with CELIAC DISEASE have problems with corn. Due to my own gluten-unrelated issues with nightshades, I stopped using potato starch.

Primarily, I use brown-rice flour and tapioca starch. For most recipes, a 50-50 blend of those two works great, although there are still some recipes for which I'm trying to find just the right ratio to achieve even better taste.

Bread is something I found a particular problem, because it's the amazing binding abilities of gluten which contribute to making wheat bread the amazing product that it is for those without gluten problems. Although I can make excellent GF chocolate-chip cookies, lemon bars, stews, soups, chili, even corn bread, I remained for a long time lost as far as making GF bread for a common sandwich. I tried mixes—in the bread machine, in the oven—mixing by hand, using a mixer, using a dough bucket; all turned out, well, decidedly unsatisfactory. While I suspected a GF bread could likely never duplicate the perfection gluten lovers experience in gluten-rich wheat bread, I kept on trying. In the meantime, there were companies that made okay, good, even really good GF bread, and I used those.

100% GF local bakeries are the best providers. Not only is their GF bread fresh, but it often doesn't have the preservatives like so many others. It's fun to walk into one and just smell its bread baking. Jonathan and the boys can inhale without worrying about the wheat flour dust in the air.

Another challenge which I had, and with which I still have to deal, is making sure people understand how vital it is for them not to not feed my boys. Some people take the gluten-intolerance of others in the very serious way it should be taken. Others, surprisingly, act like it's no big deal. Well, it IS a huge deal. My children and Jonathan's health are always on my mind. I'm amazed at how often people seem to take gluten-intolerance as less the auto-immune disorder it is. It's only those people who are always asking me, "Can your boys have ___, or ___, or ___?" who are the ones I've come completely to trust with my children's diet welfare. Those who never ask, seeming to assume they automatically know what's okay, usually don't have a clue.

Of course, by now, my boys know not to eat food other people offer them unless Kelly and Ozias first ask, "Is there gluten or wheat, or rye, or barley, or oats in this?"

I try very hard to make sure they don't ever feel socially ostracized or left out because of our GF Way. I make sure they have GF birthday cakes and GF ice-cream cones. I make sure they and their friends have GF cornbread with GF homemade chili, and provide them with a never-ending supply of tasty GF cookies and other GF goodies and desserts.

Unfortunately, many people honestly have no or very little idea of what's in the food that they eat these days. They're so into eating so much processed food that they've lost touch with what's put into that food. I, on the other hand, know exactly what goes into my meatloaf, my lemon bars, and my scalloped potatoes with ham.

Mainly, all the food we eat is made from the items in my pantry, and I cook and bake mainly from scratch. Okay, I do use, on occasion, a GF boxed mix, but that's rare. Is GF-cooking-from-scratch time consuming? Sometimes. Is it worth it? Yes! Do I see anything wrong with boxed GF mixes? Not if you have the money to buy them, they save you time, and they allow you to stay Gluten-Free.

I've included some of my favorite companies in this book's Appendix B. I have also included the names of some companies that I haven't tried, yet, but will. I love walking into a store and seeing some new GF product on the shelf to buy and try. Since more and more companies are starting up GF-product lines, I've actually gotten a bit behind in my sampling of everything presently available.

CHAPTER NINETEEN

EATING OUT THE GF WAY

I love a restaurant that accommodates GF needs. One we've been going to for years, is the 13 Coins®. We've never had a problem with its food, staff, or chef.

A meal out on the town can be made a lot less stressful when you know the restaurant you're visiting cares about you enough to do as much as it can to make sure your specific dietary needs are met.

Knowing what you eat at any restaurant, before you arrive, is always the best policy. If you can't do that, it's always worth looking at its menu to see if there are specific GF entrees. On my way to the library one day, I checked out the menu of a café I spotted a few blocks away and was pleasantly surprised to find about one-fifth of its menu was GF. It even had a GF casserole made with brown-rice pasta.

If there are no obvious GF selections, ask questions. How knowledgeable is the wait staff? For instance, you tell the server that you have specific dietary needs and ask, "What's in your creamy garlic sauce?" I would hope the response would be something like, "Our creamy garlic sauce is a blend of rich cream, freshly minced garlic, oregano, basil, parsley, and a hint of salt." What I do not want to hear is, "The garlic sauce has garlic. Oh, and it has milk." This doesn't give all of the ingredients, nor does it make the server come across as knowledgeable, let alone help ensure your food selections will be safe.

Tuna packed in water isn't necessarily *just* packed in water but a "broth" that can include two or more of the following: carrots, celery, bell peppers, and soy. Kirkland Signature® (Costco®) brand tuna *is* Gluten-Free.

Only some salad dressings are safe, while some are not. Sometimes Jonathan asks for his salad dressing "on the side," so that he can taste it to see if he has a noticeable reaction. If he doesn't, he'll only then dump the remaining dressing onto his salad. If he does react, he's happy that his entire salad isn't contaminated.

Gravies are very bad—unless you know that a thickener has been used that is Gluten-Free and that the meat broth (if it contains real meat broth) is from meat that is Gluten-Free. Unless it's a place that caters to the GF lifestyle, I would always recommend saying no to gravies and sauces; unless you are 100% sure they're safe.

Watch out for things that are breaded, too, such as fish sticks, fish fillets, chicken nuggets, chicken, fried zucchini, mozzarella sticks, corn dogs, onion rings, tater tots.... Anytime something is deep-fried, you have to watch out, as the oil may have been used previously to deep fry items that were breaded. In my opinion, if something is deep-fried after something with gluten has been deep-fried in the same oil, that oil is contaminated, and no one eating GF should eat anything deep-fried in it. I know others would disagree with me, but it only takes a very small amount of contamination for a noticeable reaction and to do damage to your body. Is it really worth the risk? For my family, it's not. We recently purchased a deep fryer and have thoroughly enjoyed the homemade corn dogs, onion rings, mozzarella sticks, French fries, sweet potato fries and fried zucchini. It has been nice to have deep-fried food without the worry of possible reaction to food-contaminated oil.

Another favorite dish that almost always has gluten in it is meatloaf. Bread crumbs, corn flakes (a lot of them have barley malt), oats (unless certified GF), croutons, and the like all have gluten. [NOTE: I've included in the Recipe section of this book my meatloaf recipe that I have tweaked and played with over the last nine or so years. It's not exactly the same every time, as I like to change ingredients here and there. Meatloaf is one dish that when I make it, there's hardly ever anything left over.]

Pies and cheesecakes with a crumb crust—that crumb crust is nine times out of ten, a graham cracker (gluten) crumb crust. That chocolate pie with the Oreos®-cookie crust? Yup—Oreos® contain gluten.

Oh and puddings—you must look out for what they are thickened with—is it corn starch, wheat flour, tapioca starch, or what?

Most cheeses are safe. However, bleu cheese and bleu-cheese dressings for a long time were not. I have heard, though, that Kraft® and Marie's® both now make a GF bleu-cheese dressing, but I haven't tried either of them—yet.

I'm loyal to establishments that answer my questions clearly, go out of their way to make sure their food is safe, and I make it known that we will be back. I love sending in letters, emails, and I always try to fill out and turn in the comment cards. If there is a survey to do on-line, or one that's on the receipt, I do that as well. I'm a firm believer in letting establishments know if I was happy or unhappy with their food, service, cleanliness, menu choices.... I'm also not afraid to leave a smaller tip or no tip at all if the service is poor—I'll also mention my opinions to the host and/or manager as well—sometimes they'll take some off of my bill to compensate for the lack of quality service.

When a local restaurant has safe GF food and an understanding management and staff, visit it often and tell everyone (whether GF or not) about it. Blog favorably about it. Email it and thank it for being on top of things by having GF items on its menu. On the other hand, if you don't like a restaurant and have constructive criticism and/or suggestions to make it more GF friendly, write its manager, owner, or chef. Changes *can* happen as the result of your input.

WILLIAM MALTESE MOMENT #8

The Long Wait

For anyone with a gluten-intolerance problem—take it from a friend who sympathizes, empathizes, and is thoroughly aware of your condition and of your constant effort to keep your health at its peak—make it a point to know a restaurant or at least its menu whenever headed out with gluten-tolerant friends or relatives for a night on the town, even if it necessitates you calling ahead.

Even I, thinking I full knew what to expect when spontaneously stopping in at a convenient eatery with my co-author and her gluten-intolerant family, found myself becoming fidgety as the process played out of their determining which items of interest on the menu were suitable for GF-Way consumption.

By the time it was decided which of the soups didn't have wheat in them, which salads didn't have croutons made of wheat bread, which servings of fish weren't contaminated by gluten-contaminated breading, which gravies and desserts weren't made with wheat-flour thickening, I was falling asleep at the table, only kept awake by gnawing hunger. I had been saved from all of that, on all previous fine-dining experiences with the same GF-Way family, by my niece or her husband merely having called beforehand to determine what was edible, as far as their non-gluten family was concerned, and what each would be ordering as soon as we arrived.

CHAPTER TWENTY

GLUTEN-FREE BAKING CLASS: HOME-MADE BREAD AT LAST!

In May 2009, I took a Gluten-Free baking class at Marlene's Market & Deli® in Federal Way, Washington. The class was taught by pastry chef Reginald E. Beck, owner of The Fearless Bread, who was kind enough to write the back-cover blurb for this book.

For me, always frustrated in being unable to bake the perfect GF bread, it was an inspiration to hear Chef Reginald relate his own struggles, as a professional, with bricks and blobs of GF dough.

It was exciting to watch him mix his resulting recipe for GF bread and see it turn out looking and tasting just as wonderful as it did.

I was made ecstatic by the possibility that I, too, his recipe in hand, might soon be able to make and bake a loaf of GF bread just as wondrous looking and as delicious as his. And, sure enough, I DID succeed, at long last, in concluding my long and often frustrating search for the perfect GF loaf—thanks to Chef Reginald and his having taken the time and made the effort to accept the challenge of GF baking. I'll always be appreciative of him for making it happen, and of Lori at Marlene's Market & Deli® for allowing him to pass on his discovery (See Recipe section in back of book) in the store-sponsored cooking class.

CHAPTER TWENTY-ONE

CREATING MY (YOUR) OWN NEW RECIPES

Since around age eight, I've been given cookbooks as gifts. You could call me a cookbook addict. Besides my more recent GF-cookbook acquisitions, I have the regular Better Homes & Gardens versions...a high-school choir cookbook...a ladies' church group cookbook.... If 99% of all regular cookbooks, including those had by me, are for gluten-rife items, I can "convert" each and every dish in them into its GF equivalent; so can you. Though I'll probably never get to all of them, I know that should I ever get in the mood for GF onion rings or GF corn dogs, I have regular recipes that, though not GF, can be used as the foundations for GF versions.

I love trying new recipes. I love experimenting with old ones. I love combining two or more recipes to make something entirely new.

One of the best compliments I can receive is someone asking me to make them their favorite of my GF recipes. As my co-author has already told you, Uncle William always asks for my husband's lasagna. Another wants my split pea soup with ham. Yet another always asks for my lemon bars. One wants my brownies, and another asks for my oatmeal cookies. I love being able to share my GF food with friends and family. Now that most of my GF recipes are pretty much just how I want them, I have less need to use people as guinea pigs (I mean as "taste-testers"). Now, I make food already judged good. I love watching people taste my food and see their look of shock (pleasant) as to how good it tastes. Gluten-Free doesn't necessarily mean taste free.

I have a journal/food notebook that includes each GF recipe I've ever made, and the variations I've performed on it. I've noted where I got the original recipe, brand names I've used by way of ingredients, temperatures at which I've cooked it, the cookware I've used, and so on. I've noted what I thought of each variation, taste-wise, and often include the comments of anyone who happened to be eating it with me at the time.

When you convert any recipe from gluten based to GF, always carefully consider what you're after by way of the following, because GF alternatives to gluten ingredients in any recipe can provide subtle or glaring differences in the final outcome:

Consistency
Color
Chewiness
Taste

Take a gluten-included recipe and read over the ingredients. On one side of a piece of paper write the recipe's original ingredients. On the opposite side write possible exchange ingredients. For example, if dairy is out, what about rice, soy, or almond milk? Personally, I love baking and cooking with rice milk, specifically Rice Dream®. Wheat-flour out, what GF flour do you think you might prefer trying in substitute? How about brown-rice flour, white-rice flour, coconut flour, acorn flour, sorghum flour, potato starch, tapioca starch, corn flour, corn meal, soy flour…?

Again, be sure to keep track in your food journal of something in the recipe that you might change that makes the end result better or worse. Note how it tastes when made of soy flour or when you used rice flour. Practice, in such cases, may not necessarily make perfect, but it will get you more and more comfortable cooking and baking the GF way.

When beginning the GF lifestyle, and for years thereafter, you'll have many learning experiences—which is how you and I should think of "failed recipes" or "flopped cakes" or "harder-than-brick-breads." I always equate those with Thomas Edison's experiences with the light bulb when he said: "I haven't failed; I've just found 10,000 ways that don't work."

Learn to go with the flow and enjoy the ride.

GF cooking and baking does require some attention to details. The more you do it, though, the easier it becomes.

I love experimenting, over and over, with recipes like the one I use for cheese fondue. Along the way, I've discovered one-inch cubes of GF Trader Joe's® Brown-Rice Bread—be careful, as it molds FAST due to lack of preservatives—is perfect; it doesn't crumble but stays on the fondue fork without going all soggy with hot cheese. I used a couple other GF breads, in subsequent tries, that didn't hold up nearly as well.

I've found Haley's Corner Bakery® Multi-Grain GF Bread perfect for bacon-lettuce-tomato (BLT) sandwiches and for egg-salad sandwiches. It has lots of grains and seeds. Their GF angle-food cake—especially chocolate—is oh-my yummy, too! Their frosted ginger cookies are delicious! Recently, I took a friend with me to Haley's. She was so impressed, she stopped right after walking in and said, "To think all of this is Gluten-Free!" She wasn't any more amazed than I was, considering I began the GF way in the days when I was lucky to find an item, here and there; never a whole bakery devoted to them.

WILLIAM MALTESE MOMENT #9

GOOD—A MATTER OF TASTE

I've been told by more than one person who converted to the GF Way that giving up gluten is like a junkie giving up his drug of choice. Someone, in fact, once told me that gluten and heroin have a very similar molecular structure.

It certainly seems as if those born into the GF Way have a better chance of adapting to it than those subjected to gluten withdrawal; what hasn't hooked you can't yet hold you. Those having never tasted the deliciousness and favorable consistencies attributed to the presence of gluten in food don't have the intact memories of late converts to the GF Way who have had extended periods of gluten exposure and a chance to be seduced to its dark-side (as regards the gluten intolerant), despite the detrimental effects it has on their health.

As someone who isn't gluten intolerant, isn't allergic to wheat or any other grain, but who has experimented with GF food not only by way of researching this book but as a general all-around healthy way to go, I speak from experience when I say that as far as GF foods have come, these past few years, there is just something about gluten-laden food that keeps drawing me back to it, time and time again.

If you're converting to the GF Way don't be fooled into believing that you're going to enter a world of tastes exactly like those you've experienced in your gluten lifestyle, because that just isn't going to happen. I'm not saying the tastes you'll encounter will be bad or not delicious, but I am saying that they will be different.

My niece mentioned her long search for the perfect GF bread, and her genuine pleasure in having had Chef Reginald provide her with her present recipe. Well, I've tasted the bread in question, and no one should eat a piece expecting it to taste exactly like its gluten-filled counterpart. Good as it is, it doesn't.

As delicious as those GF items might look in the bakery, looks can be deceptive. I've selected GF rice-flour cream puffs that looked just as light and as delicate as their gluten-laced wheat-flour cousins, only to end up with pastry so tough that I needed a pair of pliers, as well as my teeth, to dismantle it.

GF brown rice in a dish can make the finished product decidedly grainy or unappetizingly dark. Soy and bean flours can provide a decidedly annoying aftertaste. Rice flour, as already mentioned, can make things not only tough and chewy but exceedingly dry; eating rice cakes can seem like you're eating cardboard.

Just realize that if you're allergic to wheat or you're gluten intolerant, your health and general well-being are threatened by any inability by you to shift your taste preferences to the GF alternative. Even I, if faced with the alternatives of delicious wheat-flour bread and cloud-delicate cream puffs, or early death and feeling crummy, grumpy, and tired 24/7, would likely opt for eating heavier GF bread and tougher GF bakery pastry.

CHAPTER TWENTY-TWO

GLUTEN-FREE EATING IS A LIFESTYLE, NOT A DIET

There are many things to learn and remember as you launch yourself on the GF way. The only way for anyone gluten intolerant to get really healthy is to live the GF lifestyle with the right mindset. You gotta wanna! The more you live it, the more you'll come to love it. If you can't seem to get into the loving mode, please send us comments on our blog and we'll do our best to help out.

Some people see a huge difference in cost between a package of (wheat) spaghetti that costs $1-$2 and a package of rice/corn spaghetti which is anywhere from $3-$6. Money does talk, but with the cost of GF-prepared foods, money SCREAMS. Therefore, I highly suggest eating foods that are naturally Gluten-Free—lettuces, vegetables (raw, steamed, or grilled), and fruits. For hamburgers without the cost of a GF bun, use 100% beef hamburger patties with a leaf of lettuce. Or just build the burger on the plate and eat with a fork and knife (it takes a bit longer to eat and you might end up eating less chips or fries—

make sure they're GF and not deep-fried in gluten-contaminated oil).

If you view the GF way as a DIET, or a BAD-TASTE THING, you'll never truly be happy or healthy, because you'll convince yourself that it's okay to cheat, splurge, and not check labels or ask every single time you eat.

The Gluten-Free Way is not a FAD! It's not the Atkins™ diet, the South Beach diet®, a juice diet, or a low-carb diet. It is a lifestyle change, a lifestyle choice, which must occur to ensure and promote healing and to stop more damage to your body. "Diet" to most people means eating habits to promote weight loss. The GF Way isn't to lose weight; although some of you will lose weight as bodies begin to heal and actually absorb and use more minerals and vitamins...will get healthier as you feel better, good, GREAT, and become more active...will do more...will spend less time sick at home and away from school or work...will spend less time at the doctor's office....

It's awesome to watch someone go GF and see how he or she changes—sometimes losing weight...seeing improved skin...suffering less or no headaches...enjoying better moods, attitudes, and behavior...better tolerating (maybe/maybe not) dairy...suffering less gas/intestinal issues...feeling and looking better...riding a far less mood-shift emotional roller coaster...and (hopefully) fighting less with family, friends, acquaintances, and business associates.

The transformation from gluten to 100% GF is amazing in how people become genuinely healthy for probably the first time in their lives.

CHAPTER TWENTY-THREE

WHAT DO YOU MEAN *THAT* HAS GLUTEN IN IT?

The Gluten-Free Way is mostly about food. Aside from food that naturally contain gluten, there are those that have it injected, dusted on, added, and soaked in—you think of it, and I'm sure it's done.

Chicken and turkey are injected with wheat-contaminated broth. Butterball® puts "Gluten-Free" on their turkeys. "Safeway® Select Ice-Glazed Chicken Breasts" (thighs and chicken tenders) state "ice-glazed and nothing else added."

A friend brought over Fred Meyer® frozen chicken breasts for dinner. When I'd called him to ask if he'd pick up the chicken, I'd specifically said to get the Safeway® brand. He got Fred Meyer® brand instead. As a result, Jonathan and both boys got headaches and started feeling ill before we were even done with dinner. The boys looked at me—the oldest asked, "Mama, why are we sick?" I told them that the friend bought the wrong chicken. The friend said, "I didn't know there was a difference." To which I replied, "There is and this is why I specifically said, 'Get it at Safeway®.'" Since that incident, neither I nor the boys trust that friend when it comes to food.

While standing in a line at a check-out counter, I was next to a mother with her teenage daughter. The daughter grabbed some candy. The mother asked, "Did you check the ingredients?" The daughter stated she had and handed it to her mom. The mom read the label and pointed out the Allergen Statement that said, "Processed in a facility that also processes nuts, tree nuts, soy, and wheat." She told the daughter that she couldn't have it because the Mom didn't have the time to take her daughter to "the ER yet again."

There are some products I buy that have allergen statements on their labels. I always read them. They make me more confident of the company's product. Sometimes, I feel confident in buying certain products, because of what I've read on company websites. If a company makes no mention of allergens in its website's Frequently Asked Questions (FAQ) section, I don't completely trust its product. Luckily, companies have started placing higher priority on getting allergen information to the public.

I applaud companies that step up to the plate and put consumers' specific dietary needs high on their list. Those are the companies that I'm loyal to—I buy their products, I email them to thank them for putting Gluten-Free on their labels, allergen information on their websites, and for being "friendly" to those with specific dietary needs.

I try very hard not to make the GF Way come across as a disability, a big deal, or too far from the norm! My boys know that they eat non-gluten food, but I don't want them to see it as a bad or weird thing for them to do.

When people ask, "How can you live like that?" I tend to respond, "How could I continue to live with Jonathan and Kelly like they were when they ate gluten?" That part of our lives I do not ever want to repeat. It was frustrating, depressing, annoying, confusing, and costly in lack of sleep, lots of fights, tons of questions from others about why Kelly was always screaming. I look back amazed as to how I handled it as well as I did. There were days it was so difficult, what with no sleep for me, not a lot of rest for Kelly, and Jonathan exhausted from walking Kelly around the house (literally) for two to three hours almost every night. Traveling with Kelly before going GF was rare—it was so difficult.

I have no regrets about the GF Way we've chosen. I only regret not having had the foresight to press for a Celiac Disease diagnosis of Jonathan and Kelly long before I did.

Take the Gluten-Free lifestyle seriously so you can get and stay healthy. Gluten-Free doesn't mean lack of taste, lack of good ingredients, or a lack of fun. Real fun is only possible when you're healthy enough to enjoy it.

WILLIAM MALTESE MOMENT #10

Xoçai™ Chocolate

As a genuine chocolate addict and advocate of over-all healthy living, I admit to having planned, from the get-go, to plug Xoçai™ chocolate, in this non-gluten book, as a dessert, or as a chocolate option in recipes for any health-conscious person with a gluten-allergy condition—if just because I not only personally believe this particular kind of chocolate is so beneficial to my well-being, and can be to yours, but because I'm not alone in that belief, backed up by the results of scientific studies like those conducted by, Eliot Brinton, M.D., University of Utah, on blood pressure, glucose, insulin, lipids, and other risk factors that affect the cardiovascular system.

As someone with a history of Type II Diabetes in his family, I had my blood glucose levels spike dangerously high during my mother's long period of dying from ovarian cancer, when I had the weighty responsibility of being her sole caregiver. While, since her death, my glucose levels have receded, undoubtedly accountable to a lessening of stress, I still monitor my blood sugar on a regular basis. Time after time, I've discovered that consumption of regular chocolate can send my blood glucose above recommended levels, while consumption of the same amount of Xoçai™ chocolate keeps it confined within prescribed safety limits.

That said, my original intention was to recommend the chocolate Xoçai™ XoBiotic™ Squares *and* Xoçai™ MEGA Squares, since those are my favorites. While the company offers a whole array of additional items, including cookies, health bars, and even a drink, I'm not as particularly fond of those and, besides, many of them contain gluten.

Luckily, as I was busy thinking about what to write here—by way of recommending Xoçai™ chocolate of which I seemingly can't eat enough, as well as devising at least a couple of recipes that incorporate them in non-gluten desserts for your sweet-tooth dining pleasure (see Recipe section at end of book)—I did what my co-author, and I, and our book, steadfastly recommend *you always do*: I checked the back of my Xoçai™ boxes for "Allergy info," and am glad I did. While my very favorite Xoçai™ XoBiotic™ Squares gave me the go-ahead with, "Processed in a plant that uses peanuts and treenuts," the MEGA Squares surprised with "May contain peanuts, tree nuts, and/or WHEAT" (the capitalization mine).

That sent me off to the Xoçai™ web-site, where this popped up:

"The Nuggets, the X Power Squares, XoBiotic™ Squares, and the Omega Squares are considered Gluten-Free because there is no ingredient that contains gluten. The remaining products do contain wheat (gluten). The solid chocolate products are, however, produced on the

same machines as other products that contain gluten. These machines are cleaned thoroughly after each production, but we legally need to include the allergy warning because of this."

This means that my co-author might not let her family near Xoçai™, and that every one else intent upon a GF-Way of life should be just as cautious, maybe sampling a small amount of chocolate at a time to test the possibilities, minor as they may be, of cross-contamination reactions.

For more information, go to the official Xoçai™ website or to the website I've specifically set up for selling this chocolate:

http://www.mxi.myvoffice.com/williammaltese

CHAPTER TWENTY-FOUR

MY 100% GLUTEN-FREE WAY IDEA OF A GOOD TIME

We went into G.F. Joe's Market® in Tumwater, Washington. Right after we walked in, I saw the Grand Pasta Shells by Tinkyada® that we haven't been able to find anywhere in almost four years. They had numerous other brands that I'd never heard of before. They had different shapes, different grains, from lots of different companies.

I was like a kid in a candy store!

They had two freezers full of GF—frozen breads, pizza crusts, desserts, waffles, cookie dough, pie crusts, and dinner rolls. Another freezer had pre-made GF pizzas and desserts. The aisles were full of GF sauces, mixes, flours, granolas, chips, cookies, spices, cereals, and pretzels. They stock over 1,300 different items, including GF ice-cream cones and GF decorator sprinkles (without artificial coloring).

They carry a small but wide selection of GF books. They bring in GF products from two bakeries we love:

Sunny Valley Wheat Free® (in Maple Valley, Washington) and Haley's Corner Bakery® (in Kent, Washington).

We had a nice chat with the owners of G.F. Joe's Market®, Joe and Kaylee. It was fun to swap "so how long have *you* been GF?" stories.

I love walking into a store and having my boys hear, "Everything here is Gluten-Free." It's a breath of fresh air! My boys don't have to be afraid to touch items on the shelves, because there's no gluten to make them sick. They can even eat the food samples and not have to be afraid.

Even though G.F. Joe's Market® in Tumwater is a bit of a drive from my house, I'm more than willing to go the extra distance and shop there. It's a GF family-owned business, carries practically every GF thing I need, and its customer service can't be beat!

CHAPTER TWENTY-FIVE

GLUTEN-FREE GARDENING

We have a huge garden with accompanying compost pile.

Since a lot about gluten and how it affects everything is still unknown, we have the strict rule that our garden, like everything else in our lives, be 100% Gluten-Free, including soil additives, and anything added to the compost.

We don't want Jonathan or the boys to touch anything gluten while gardening. Although there are people who disagree with me, I know from personal family experience, that negative reactions can occur just from the touching.

Another reason we garden is it helps save on our food budget. GF food is expensive for a family of four and adds up quickly. By enjoying personally grown GF greens, fresh corn-on-the-cob, and fruit, we're better able to afford store-bought GF flour and pasta, as well as GF meat and dairy. A big harvest may not happen every time, like the year it kept snowing through April, but every little bit helps.

CHAPTER TWENTY-SIX

GLUTEN AND RELIGIOUS OBSERVANCES

An area many people may not even consider as providing a danger of gluten exposure is the observance of certain religious sacraments. While some parishes and congregations allow a GF substitute, those that don't have alienated more than one church member who has decided to "move on" rather than be discriminated against because of health reasons beyond his or her control.

Luckily, the powers that be in my family's church have worked with us in allowing us not only to bring our own GF substitutes but to ensure no cross-contamination occurs.

CHAPTER TWENTY-SEVEN

OTHER DO'S AND DON'TS

Do check every label every time. Manufactures change recipes whenever they deem it necessary. For example, one type of bagged cereal used to contain no wheat, and then it did.

Do anticipate that you may not have a lot of choices at family functions, church socials, work potlucks, parties, and most restaurants. A little bit of time and preparation means you can make the most of it.

Do enjoy the GF lifestyle—no pills, no icky liquids, and no needles. Just different grains.

Do plan ahead. Keep GF snacks in the car. A snack before a party will help keep the hunger pains at bay, especially if the food selection mainly contains gluten.

Do prepare yourself for the possible confrontations with family members, especially at the holidays. Traditions are not always easily broken or changed, so beware that offering a GF dish may raise heated concerns.

Do tip generously for service and GF needs being met.

Do volunteer. Help out with your local GF-support group.

- **Do** join a GF-support group. Being around others that live the GF lifestyle will strengthen your resolve not to cheat, learn of new products, and help others along the GF Way.
- **Do** take a breath and remember that it takes time to learn all the facets of the GF way of life.
- **Do** encourage family and friends to make GF foods for you. If you fear cross-contamination issues, at the beginning, invite them over to help you make the food.
- **Do** your best not to cheat and eat gluten. Cheating hurts you. Cheating also shows others that you're not taking your health seriously.
- **Do** realize that you will not learn everything GF over night or in a weekend.
- **Do** read books on CELIAC DISEASE, GF lifestyle, and GF cooking—like this one. Knowledge is power—the power to be strong and fight the urge to cheat.
- **Do** call and check websites of manufacturers about the products you want to eat and use. Patronize the ones that list GF status on their sites. Write or email the companies that have knowledgeable staff that can answer your GF concerns. Share what you learn with others at GF support groups, email lists, blogs, and by word of mouth.
- **Do** keep track of what you eat and use—especially at the beginning. A food you think is safe may not be—so "track" your consumption of it to see if a reaction pattern shows up.
- **Do** be sure to list your gluten intolerance on ALL doctor forms—primary care doctor, eye doctor, dentist, hospi-

tal, physical therapist, and so on. Make sure your chart is marked with the appropriate "Allergy Alert" flag.

Do educate your doctor and other medical professionals that are part of your health care team.

Do be sure the people at your place of employment know of your gluten-intolerance, and that the people at your children's school know of your children's gluten intolerance—in case of emergency.

Do suggest more healthy alternatives for consumption in the workplace. Offer to bring a GF fruit tray to replace those dozen donuts. Suggest a GF veggie platter instead of bagels and cream cheese.

Do remind yourself that the GF life means a healthy life.

Do remind yourself that you are doing this for YOU and for YOUR health and for YOUR FAMILY'S well-being.

Do educate yourself.

Do ask stores to carry the GF products you want to buy.

Do try to taste each and every GF product at least once. Keep a list of your likes and dislikes.

Do thank anyone who tries to help meet your GF needs.

Do educate family and friends. Start small—a pan of GF brownies to share. Let them eat some before mentioning its ingredients.

Do offer to bring a GF dish or two to functions. Offer to bring GF dishes that, otherwise, are most likely to contain gluten—like macaroni salad, cornbread, most desserts, pasta salads, enchiladas....

Don't expect people to understand your GF dietary restrictions—most won't, at least not at first.

- **Don't** be afraid to stand up for your GF health in any situation.
- **Don't** assume that anyone truly understands your GF health needs, no matter how many times you explain them.
- **Don't** assume that just because a restaurant has a GF menu, that cross-contamination is a non-issue. There's always a possibility of cross-contamination. Really, the only safe places are probably those that are 100% GF.
- **Don't** assume that anyone has your GF needs in your best interest. It's not always that easy.
- **Don't** believe everything you see on food labels. There have been times when, according to the label, the food seemed safe, but after eating the food, my husband and kids all reacted.
- **Don't** expect others to remember your GF needs 100% of the time.
- **Don't** plan on always finding GF food wherever you may be—especially when traveling—so be prepared.

WILLIAM MALTESE MOMENT #11

ONE MORE DON'T TO DO

Don't, even for one brief moment, ever think that you are completely alone and helpless in your wandering through a predominantly gluten- and/or wheat-tolerant environment. You are, in fact, but one of thousands already identified, with likely thousands more about to be found, as more and more facts of these immune-system conditions are made known to those who are known to have them and to those who, now, inadvertently have them.

While I was aware of the condition, due to my niece's family's dealings with it, and genuinely thought this book would find a significant niche and provide resonance with enough readers to make it worthwhile, it was only while writing the book that I've become truly cognizant of just how wide-spread the condition is. My mere mention of my involvement in this project brought in such a flood of response from gluten- and wheat-intolerant people, worldwide, that I can well understand why a lot of the major food producers are now finding it lucrative enough, by way of company profit margins, to provide products especially for non-gluten buyers.

So, don't think that by having recognized and discovered your allergy to gluten and wheat that you've summoned Armageddon to your doorstep. Breathe deeply, look around, do your research, take advantage of newly provided GF food for your menu, find others facing the same dietary challenges as yourself, create a loan/ exchange library of books on GF living and cooking with others, so you don't have to buy every book in the store, and keep right on truckin'. The 100% Gluten-Free Way isn't the easiest road to travel, but you can, with just a bit of effort, maneuver its each and every obstacle and speed bump to find yourself, surprisingly soon, not only feeling far healthier but likely transformed into someone far different and far better, in disposition, and well-being, than when you first began your journey.

Bon voyage! And do enjoy your trip of discovery and recovery!

GLUTEN-FREE RECIPES

NOTE

Part of the fun of the Gluten-Free Way is experimenting with different flours to find what you like best. There are many flours to choose from and each has its pros and cons. There is no such thing as a failed recipe—just one that you won't repeat. Keep track of your experiments so that you can repeat the yummy ones and avoid making the bricks and blobs accidentally a second (or a third) time. Enjoy the Gluten-Free lifestyle.

Bon Appétit!

► *Desserts*

FLOURLESS CHOCOLATE TORTE: PAVÉ JOSEPHINE

(Gluten-Free Version by "Torte Man" from Pure Chocolate, by Fran Bigelow)

1¼ pounds of semi-sweet chocolate, finely chopped
½ pound of unsalted butter (two sticks) room temperature
6 large eggs at room temperature

Note: Measurements must be exact—too much or too little and it won't turn out.

Put rack in middle of oven. Preheat to 300 F. Butter 9-inch round cake pan and place parchment circle in bottom. In double boiler, melt chocolate on low heat. Remove from heat when chocolate is almost melted and stir until smooth. Add butter in three parts, stirring until you don't see butter anymore. If butter begins to melt and separate, let chocolate cool a little bit (as the butter is being heated too quickly). Mixture should be glossy and smooth—no lumps. Set aside until mixture is like softened butter. Return to double boiler if it begins to thicken too much.

Put whisk on electric mixer, and beat eggs at medium speed for 5-6 minutes until light and triple in volume. Take egg mixture (about ⅓) and fold into chocolate. Take rest of mixture and fold into chocolate. Pour mixture into prepared pan. Place pan on a cookie sheet with sides, and pour enough water onto cookie sheet so there is about ½ inch.

Bake about 30-35 minutes. Top should be dull but center will look set and be shiny. When shaken, it should jiggle slightly. Take out and let set for 2 hours. Take a thin blade and run it around the edge of the cake and invert it onto a plate. Then, turn it back over and let it rest on parchment paper. Wrap up and put into fridge until ready to serve. When ready to serve, bring to room temperature and remove parchment paper.

Options for serving: Sift a small amount of powder sugar on top. Drizzle with chocolate glaze. Dollop some whipped cream on top. With an accompanying tall glass of milk. (Adrienne's personal favorite).

Bonnie's Xocai™ XoBiotic™ Chocolate and Strawberries Zabaglione

(Gluten-Free Version by William Maltese)[1]

¼ cup of heavy cream
½ cup chopped Xoçai™ XoBiotic™ Squares

Heat cream over medium heat until about 105 F. degrees. In the meantime, put the chocolate pieces in a glass bowl. Add the warm cream and put over a hot water, not boiling bath—not touching the bottom of the bowl. Take off the heat. Stir until chocolate is melted. Keep warm.

8 egg yolks
⅔ cup sugar
½ cup dry Marsala wine
pinch of salt

Blend the egg yolks, sugar, Marsala, and salt with a whisk in a large glass bowl until blended. Put the bowl over simmering water, not touching the bottom of the bowl, and whisk until thick and creamy, about 5 minutes. Remove from heat. Let cool until warm. Fold the melted chocolate mixture into the egg mixture.

1 lb. of strawberries, quartered

---

[1] While this Xoçai™ product is labeled Gluten-Free, it is prepared in the same machines as prepares gluten products. Though the machines are thoroughly cleaned after each production, the possibility for cross-contamination should be considered.

Divide the strawberries into 6 dessert dishes. Pour the chocolate mixture over the strawberries, and serve.

BONNIE'S XOÇAI™ XOBIOTIC™ CHOCOLATE TIRAMISU

(Gluten-Free Version by William Maltese)[2]

Part #1:

2 tablespoons whipping cream, or heavy cream
¼ cup Xoçai™ XoBiotic™ Chocolate* squares, chopped
4 large egg yolks
⅓ cup sugar
¼ cup dry Marsala wine
pinch salt

Part #2:

6 ounces of mascarpone cheese
⅔ cup whipping cream
½ cup sugar
chilled results of part #1 (see above)

---

[2] While this Xoçai™ product is labeled Gluten Free, it is prepared in the same machines as prepares gluten products. Though the machines are thoroughly cleaned after each production, the possibility for cross-contamination should be considered.

2½ cups espresso coffee, warmed (or coffee-flavored liqueur)
24 crisp Gluten-Free ladyfinger cookies
unsweetened cocoa powder, for garnish
shavings from Xoçai™ XoBiotic™ Chocolate squares for garnish

Prepare part #1 by heating cream in a heavy saucepan over medium heat until it reaches a temperature of 110 F. degrees. Add chocolate and stir until chocolate is melted. Set aside and keep warm.

Whisk the egg yolks, sugar, Marsala, and salt in a large glass bowl until blended. Set the bowl over a saucepan of simmering water, but do not allow the bottom of the bowl to touch the water. Whisk the egg mixture over the simmering water until it is thick and creamy, about 4 minutes. Remove from the heat. Cool to 110 F. degrees.

Using a large rubber spatula, fold the melted chocolate mixture into the egg mixture. Cover and refrigerate to chill completely.

Prepare part #2 by placing the mascarpone cheese in a large bowl and set aside.

With an electric mixer, beat the cream and ¼ cup of the sugar in a medium bowl until soft peaks form. Fold the whipped cream into the mascarpone. Then fold in chilled results of part #1. Cover and refrigerate.

Whisk the warmed espresso and the remaining ¼ cup of sugar in another medium bowl until blended. Line a 9¼-inch by 5 x 2¾-inch metal loaf pan with plastic wrap, allowing the plastic to extend over the sides. Working with

1 cookie at a time, dip 8 cookies into the espresso and arrange in a single layer side by side over the bottom of the prepared pan. Spoon ⅓ of the mascarpone mixture over the cookies to cover.

Repeat dipping 8 of the cookies in the espresso and layering the cookies and remaining mascarpone mixture 2 more times. Dip the remaining 8 cookies in the espresso and arrange side by side atop the tiramisu. Press lightly to compact slightly (the last layer will extend above the pan sides). Cover with plastic and refrigerate at least 6 hours.

Unwrap the plastic from atop the tiramisu. Invert the tiramisu onto a platter. Remove the plastic. Sift the cocoa over the tiramisu, and with a vegetable peeler or sharp knife, make shavings from Xoçai™ XoBiotic™ chocolate squares and sprinkle over top.

BONNIE'S XOÇAI™ XOBIOTIC™ CHOCOLATE S'MORES

(Gluten-Free Version by William Maltese)[3]

1 large Gluten-Free marshmallow
1 Gluten-Free graham cracker (like Jo-Sef®)
1 (or more) square(s) of Xoçai™ XoBiotic™ Chocolate

---

[3] While this Xoçai™ product is labeled Gluten-Free, it is prepared in the same machines as prepares gluten products. Though the machines are thoroughly cleaned after each production, the possibility for cross-contamination should be considered.

Place marshmallow into a microwavable dish. Microwave for 45 seconds, or to suitable softness. (This may vary according to your own microwave.) Sandwich the chocolate square(s) and the softened marshmallow between two pieces of cracker.

Squeeze to desirable compactness, and wait until it cools somewhat before eating.

BONNIE'S XOÇAI™ XOBIOTIC™ CHOCOLATE FLOURLESS MOLTEN CAKE

(Gluten-Free Version by William Maltese)[4]

¼ cup heavy cream
4 oz Xoçai™ XoBiotic™ Chocolate, chopped
3 egg yolks
2 Tablespoons sugar
2 teaspoon butter (for coating ramekins)

Heat cream in a heavy sauce pan to a temperature of not more than 110 F. Add Xoçai™ XoBiotic™ chocolate and beat until it melts and is shiny. Whip egg yolks with the sugar until sugar is dissolved. Fold egg mixture into chocolate mixture, mixing well.

---

[4] While this Xoçai™ product is labeled Gluten-Free, it is prepared in the same machines as prepares gluten products. Though the machines are thoroughly cleaned after each production, the possibility for cross-contamination should be considered.

Pour into two buttered 6-oz. ramekins. Bake at 300 F. for 14 to 18 minutes. Oven temperatures do vary so edges should start to form, but center will still be soft. Do NOT overcook! Carefully run a knife around the edge of ramekin to remove contents. Serve immediately.

Serves two.

DEBRA KAISER'S BREAKFAST CAKE

(Gluten-Free Version by Adrienne Z. Milligan)

1 cup butter
4 eggs
1¾ cup sugar
1 cup white-rice flour
1 cup brown-rice flour
1 cup tapioca starch
½ tsp baking powder

Mix the above ingredients. Spread ⅔ in jelly-roll pan—swirl 1 can of cherry pie filling on top. Then, spoon remaining batter on top of filling. Bake at 350 F. for 25-30 minutes. Drizzle with icing of your choice.

BANANA NUT MUFFINS

(From a recipe handed out at GF-Baking Class taught by the Fearless Bread Chef, Reginald Beck)

2 cups Gluten-Free all-purpose flour mix
⅔ cup sugar

1 Tablespoon baking powder
1 teaspoon baking soda
¾ teaspoon xanthan gum
¼ teaspoon salt
1 teaspoon cinnamon
1 packed cup ripe chopped bananas (about 2 medium bananas)
½ cup chopped walnuts, optional
2 large eggs
½ cup milk
½ cup canola oil
granulated sugar for garnishment, optional

Place rack in center of oven and preheat to 350 F. Grease muffin tin with cooking spray or use pastry brush and brush shortening into each tin. Mix flour, sugar, baking powder, baking soda, xanthan gum, salt, and cinnamon in large mixing bowl. Add bananas and walnuts and stir to coat evenly.

Combine milk and oil in small bowl, remove 1 Tablespoon of combined liquid and discard it. Beat in eggs. Add liquids to bananas and stir until just blended. Fill muffin pans ⅔ full. Bake 18-25 minutes until golden brown. Remove from pan and serve immediately or cool on a rack.

Tips: Bring all ingredients to room temperature before using. Mix the wet and dry ingredients only until they are combined; fold them together instead of beating and the end product will not be tough.

Olive's Big Pan Brownies

(Gluten-Free version by Adrienne Z. Milligan and William Maltese)

¾ cup unsweetened cocoa powder
¾ cup oil
4 eggs
2 cups sugar
½ teaspoon salt
1 teaspoon Gluten-Free vanilla
½ cup brown-rice flour
½ cup tapioca starch
1 cup nuts (optional)

Beat eggs, gradually adding the sugar, until well blended. Add the unsweetened cocoa powder, oil, salt, and vanilla. Stir in the flours and nuts. Spoon into greased 9 x 13-inch pan. Bake at 350 F. for 35-40 minutes.

Byron's Oatmeal Cookies

(Gluten-Free version by Adrienne Z. Milligan)

½ cup brown-rice flour
½ cup tapioca starch
½ teaspoon salt
½ teaspoon cloves
½ cup shortening or butter
2 Tablespoons milk
½ cup raisins or Craisins® (optional)

1 teaspoon Gluten-Free vanilla
½ teaspoon baking soda
1 teaspoon cinnamon
1 cup brown sugar
1 egg
1½ cups Gluten-Free oatmeal
½ cup nuts (optional)
1 teaspoon xanthan gum

Cream together the shortening and brown sugar. Add the dry ingredients (except the xanthan gum). Mix. Add the milk, vanilla, and egg. After everything is mixed well, add xanthan gum, oats and raisins (Craisins®, or nuts). Bake at 350 F. for 12-15 minutes.

Makes 3 dozen.

Note 1: Original recipe did not call for nuts.

Note 2: If desired, add ¼ cup Gluten-Free chocolate chips and reduce raisins or Craisins® to ¼ cup and add when adding the oats.

Note 3: When I bake these, I use either a silicone baking mat or spray the cookie sheet with a Gluten-Free non-stick cooking spray.

Note 4: Baking time will depend on size of cookies and oven. I make smaller cookies and it only takes about 9 minutes per pan.

VICTOR'S PEANUT BUTTER COOKIES[5]

1 egg
1 cup sugar
1 cup peanut butter
optional—additional sugar for coating

Mix first 3 ingredients; let rest in fridge for awhile. Make balls—whatever size balls you like (based on whatever size cookies you want); if desired, roll in sugar (I prefer without), place on baking sheet, press down with tines of a fork in cross-hatch pattern. Bake at 350 F. for 10-15 minutes, or just until they've browned (oven times may vary).

CHOCOLATE DROP FUDGE COOKIES, NO BAKE

(Gluten-Free version by Adrienne Z. Milligan)

4 Tablespoons unsweetened cocoa powder
½ cup milk
dash of salt
½ cup butter
2 cups sugar
⅛ teaspoon cream of tarter

Boil the preceding ingredients for 3 minutes. Remove from heat and add:

---

[5] Victor J. Banis has edited the cookbook *The Pot Thickens: Recipes from Writers*, available from Wildside Press/Borgo Press.

2 teaspoons Gluten-Free vanilla
3 cups Gluten-Free oats

Mix well. Spoon onto wax paper or foil and refrigerate until set.

JELL-O® COOKIES

(Gluten-Free version by Adrienne Z. Milligan and William Maltese)

3 egg whites
3½ Tablespoons or ½ package of raspberry Jell-O®
¾ cup sugar
dash of salt
1 teaspoon white vinegar
1 small package (6 ounces) Gluten-Free chocolate chips

Preheat oven to 250 F. Beat egg whites, adding Jell-O® and sugar slowly until stiff peaks form. Add salt, vinegar, and chocolate chips.

Drop by heaping teaspoon onto cookie sheet that has been covered with brown paper bag (or brown paper from a roll). Keep remaining batter in fridge.

Put in oven on bottom rack. Bake for 20 minutes. Turn off heat. Leave cookies in oven until oven cools completely. Repeat until all batter is used.

Make sure to check ingredients in Jell-O® and chocolate chips to make sure the ones used are Gluten-Free.

Grandma Pease's Cookies

(Gluten-Free version by Adrienne Z. Milligan)

2 cups white sugar
1 cup shortening (not oil) or butter or margarine
2 eggs
½ cup melted unsweetened chocolate
2 teaspoons baking powder
½ teaspoon cinnamon
½ teaspoon salt
a scant cup of milk
flour—start at 5 cups—2½ cups brown-rice flour, 2½ cups tapioca starch
additional flour (as needed)—1 cup at a time—½ cup brown-rice flour, ½ cup tapioca starch

Preheat oven to 350 F. Mix all of the ingredients but the flour.

Slowly mix in the first 5 cups of flour, and check dough consistency. Dough should pull away from the bowl. If dough doesn't pull away from the bowl, slowly add enough of the additional flour mixture until it does. To better monitor dough consistency, and avoid over-mixing, at this stage, mix by hand and not by electric mixer.

Set aside two small bowls—one with water, one with white sugar. Roll dough in hand about the size of a walnut. Dip leading half of ball into the water, then into the sugar. Place non-sugared side on cookie sheet. Press cookie down with fingers.

Bake 10 minutes.

Lemon Dream Bars

(Gluten-Free version by Adrienne Z. Milligan)

Crust:

1-cup soft butter or margarine
dash of salt
½ cup powdered sugar
1 cup brown-rice flour
1 cup tapioca starch

Combine above with pastry blender. Press into 9 x 13-inch pan. Bake 15 minutes at 350 F. degrees.

Filling:

4 eggs, beaten
Stir in 2 cups sugar
¼ cup tapioca starch
6 T. lemon juice (fresh lemon juice may give better flavor)

Pour filling into slightly cooled crust. Bake at 350 F. degrees for 20-30 minutes. When cooled, sprinkle with powdered sugar.

Pumpkin Bars

(Gluten-Free version by Adrienne Z. Milligan)

4 eggs, brought to room temperature
1⅔ cups sugar
scant cup of oil
16-ounce can of pumpkin

Beat above ingredients till light and fluffy.

Add:

½ cup brown-rice flour
½ cup tapioca starch
1 teaspoon salt
1 teaspoon baking soda
2 Tablespoons baking powder
1½ teaspoons cinnamon
1½ teaspoons nutmeg
1 cup chopped nuts, optional

Mix well. Spread in ungreased 10 x 15-inch jellyroll pan. Bake at 350 F. for 25-30 minutes.

Frosting:

3 ounces cream cheese at room temperature
1 cup powdered sugar
¼ cup margarine, softened

This makes a soft, rather runny type of frosting—not thick at all. Once the pan is cool, drizzle frosting all over. Serve warm or cool.

▶ *Cheese*

CHEESE WAFERS

(Gluten-Free Version by Adrienne Z. Milligan from Kellogg's Cheese Wafer Recipe)

¼ cup brown-rice flour
¼ cup white-rice flour
¼ cup tapioca starch
½ teaspoon salt
dash of cayenne pepper
½ cup margarine, softened (one stick—do not use butter)
2 cups (about 8 ounces, when ungrated) of shredded cheddar cheese (I prefer extra sharp)
1½ cups of Erewhon's® Crispy Rice Gluten-Free cereal (or any other Gluten-Free crispy rice cereal—I prefer the brand mentioned as it tastes and looks most to me like Kellogg's® Rice Krispies)

Preheat oven to 350 F. Combine the flours, salt, and pepper; then set aside. Beat together margarine and cheese until light and fluffy. Add flour mixture, mixing until well blended. Stir in cereal. [Note: Sometimes, it's easiest just to use your hands in order to get the cereal all mixed in.]

Using your hands, roll bits of the mixture into balls (size according to what you desire by way of cookie size). Place balls on ungreased cookie sheet. Flatten balls with a fork dipped in tapioca starch or rice flour.

Bake for 12 minutes, or until lightly browned around edges. Remove immediately from baking sheets. Cool on wire racks.

Makes approximately 5 dozen.

Note: If you would like to make bars instead of wafers, place entire mixture into a 9 x 13-inch pan and use wax paper to press firmly into pan. Bake at same temperature for 15 minutes, then rotate pan and bake for another 7-15 minutes, depending on oven. When cooled, cut and serve.

Store in airtight container.

These are a family favorite and don't last long.

ZABBY'S GRILLED CHEESE SANDWICH

2 slices GF bread (Zabby prefers the GF Sandwich Bread from Fearless Bread Chef)
cheddar cheese, pepper jack cheese, Colby jack, etc.
mayonnaise
mustard
non-stick cooking spray

Preheat griddle or skillet on medium (medium-low if using a cast iron pan). Spread one side of two slices of bread with mayonnaise (to taste, also will help moisten extra dry GF breads) and swirl some mustard (to taste) on the same side of one or both slices. Place two or three thin slices of cheese on the mayonnaise- and mustard-spread side of one slice. Put the second slice, mayonnaise- and mustard-spread side face-down, on top of the cheese-piled first slice. Spray one half of the sandwich with the non-stick cooking spray and place that side onto the heated griddle or skillet.

Once the sandwich is on griddle, and the down side is browned to your liking, spray the side that's up with the non-stick cooking spray and flip the sandwich. Cook the remaining side until cheese is melted and/or the whole sandwich is browned to your liking.

<u>Lasagna</u>

(Gluten-Free Version by Jonathan B. Milligan from recipe on box of Tinkyada Lasagna Sheets)

9 lasagna sheets
1 Tablespoon olive oil
½ teaspoon salt
½ teaspoon chopped oregano leaves
1 pound ground beef
1½ cup diced mushrooms
⅓ cup 2% milk
8 ounces shredded mozzarella cheese
2 teaspoons crushed garlic
¼ teaspoon pepper
¾ cup diced onions
1½ cup ricotta cheese
3 cans (8 ounces each) of tomato sauce

⅓ cup grated parmesan cheese

Cook rice pasta according to directions. Rinse with cold water and drain well. Brown ground beef and onions in oil. When the meat is half cooked, add mushrooms, garlic, salt, pepper, and oregano. Once meat mixture is totally cooked, drain grease. Set aside.
Preheat oven to 350F.
In a small bowl, mix ricotta cheese and milk until smooth. In an ungreased baking pan (13 x 9 x 2-inch) or baking dish (11¾ x 7½ x 1¾-inch), pour ⅓ tomato sauce onto the bottom of the pan.
Place 3 lasagna sheets on top of the sauce. Add half of the meat mixture. Next add half of the ricotta mixture. Add half of the mozzarella and half of the parmesan cheese over the top.
Repeat with ⅓ sauce, 3 lasagna sheets, rest of meat mixture, rest of ricotta mixture, and the mozzarella cheese. Add remaining lasagna sheets, tomato sauce, and top with remaining parmesan cheese.
Cover and bake for 30 minutes.
Note from Jonathan: I like to use a lint-free towel to lay out the lasagna noodles to drain. I also like to add fresh basil and parsley in addition to the oregano. I always add more mozzarella cheese (a pound per pan), as well as parmesan cheese, than are listed in the recipe. Also, I buy the big container of ricotta cheese and split it between two pans—it's more than 1½ cups per pan, but I love cheese; since discovering I'm not lactose-intolerant but gluten-intolerant, I can now eat however much cheese I want.

Dave's Tuna Mac & Cheese

1 box of Trader Joe's® Rice Pasta and cheddar cheese
1 can of tuna, drained
milk and butter, per pasta directions

Cook rice pasta according to package directions. Drain pasta and return to pot. Add cheese mixture. Stir in drained tuna.

    This is an easy meal and the tuna provides protein without preparing a separate dish.

Elaine's Cheese/Tuna Melts

Gluten-Free bread (as many slices as you want) [Note: Although Gluten-Free bread is naturally more dry than gluten bread, you may still want to pre-toast your GF bread slices to assure they don't get soggy if the filling below can't be drained completely].
canned tuna, drained
mayonnaise
garlic powder, to taste (optional)
onion powder, to taste (optional)
olives, drained and diced (optional)
crushed pineapple, drained
slices of cheddar cheese (or pepper jack, Colby jack, etc.)

Turn on oven broiler. Mix tuna with mayonnaise, garlic powder, and onion powder. Stir in olives. Spoon tuna mixture onto (pre-toasted) bread slices that have been placed on cookie sheet. (The number of slices the tuna mixture will cover depends upon how much mayonnaise used, how much is put on each slice, and how many slices there are to cover.)

After all bread is topped with tuna mixture, spoon drained crushed pineapple onto each slice of bread. Again, how much put on and how many slices determine how far it will go. Top each piece of bread with a slice (or two, or more, depending upon the size of bread and cheese) of cheese.

Put in oven under broiler until cheese is melted and slightly browned.

Vikki's Cheese Goulash

1 pound of ground beef
1 large onion, chopped
salt, pepper, and garlic powder (not garlic salt), to taste
1 teaspoon chopped parsley
2 boxes of Trader Joe's® GF Rice Pasta & Cheddar Cheese
1 can of corn, drained
1 pat of butter (not margarine)
Half a container of Imagine's® Gluten-Free tomato soup at room temperature

Cook ground beef and onion with salt, pepper, garlic powder, and parsley. Drain and set aside.

Cook pasta according to directions on box. When making cheese sauce only, though, use ¾ of total milk called for in package directions.

Once pasta has been drained, return to pot and stir in cheese sauce. Then add cooked meat, cooked onion, butter, corn, and tomato soup. Stir and reheat on low until heated through.

Note from Adrienne: This may sound weird—making Mac & Cheese then adding beef AND tomato soup. Weird it may sound, but so delicious! Thanks to Vikki, this is now a favorite.

<u>Cheese- and Asparagus-Stuffed Chicken Breasts</u>

chicken breasts, thawed (as many as you want to prepare)
cheese, shredded—about a handful per chicken breast (cheddar, mozzarella, etc.)
asparagus, rinsed and ends cut off (2 or 3 per chicken breast)

Preheat oven to 350 F. Place a piece of foil (shiny side down) on a jelly-roll pan. Slice chicken breasts as a butterfly fillet. Place most of cheese and asparagus in the middle of each breast. Roll up the sides of the chicken breasts and use toothpicks to keep the breasts and stuffing rolled.

Place all on the pan and put remaining cheese on top of the breasts. Sprinkle (if desired) the top of each breast with freshly ground black pepper, onion powder, garlic powder, and a tiny amount of salt.

Bake for 30 minutes or until chicken tests done.

Chicken breasts can be served with rice, potatoes, or GF pasta.

► *Meat*

CORN DOGS

(Gluten-Free Version by Adrienne Z. Milligan from *Better Homes and Gardens New Cookbook*'s Corn Dogs)

1 1-pound package of GF hot dogs (8 to 10)
1 cup corn flour*
⅔ cup cornmeal
2 Tablespoons sugar
1½ teaspoons baking powder
½ teaspoon dry mustard
1 beaten egg (bring egg to room temperature, then beat)
¾ cup milk
2 Tablespoons cooking oil
xanthan gum (as/if needed)
wooden skewers (if desired)
shortening or cooking oil for deep-fat frying

Preheat deep-fat fryer to 375 F. If using a large skillet, heat oil to 375 F. Pat dry hot dogs with paper towels. If desired, insert a wooden skewer (or wooden craft stick) into one end of each hot dog. Set aside.

Combine flour, cornmeal, sugar, baking powder, and dry mustard. Combine egg, milk, and the 2 Tablespoons oil. Add milk mixture to dry ingredients and mix well. Batter will be thick. If batter is super runny, add xanthan gum. Begin with no more than ¼ teaspoon. Mix in well and then let set at least five minutes. Stir again. If it is still too runny, add another ¼ teaspoon of xanthan gum. It shouldn't take much xanthan gum, if at all. Each time I mix it, it varies.

The easiest way I've found to coat the hot dogs is to pour the batter into a tall glass. Coat each hot dog with batter by dipping. Place each coated hot dog into deep-fat fryer or skillet. Turn with tongs after 10 seconds to prevent the batter from sliding off.

Cook 3 minutes more; turn again after 1½ minutes. Serve with ketchup and mustard, if desired.

Serves 4 or 5.

Note: sometimes I use ½ cup corn flour, ¼ cup tapioca starch, and ¼ cup rice bran for a different flavor and texture.

SHANGHAI CHICKEN WINGS

(Gluten-Free Version by Adrienne Z. Milligan)

2 pounds Gluten-Free chicken wings (can also use drumsticks, breasts, strips)—works with thawed or frozen
⅓ cup Gluten-Free soy sauce
⅓ cup water
2 Tablespoons sugar
2 slices fresh ginger root (can also use powdered ginger)

2 cloves garlic, smashed

Cut tips from chicken wings and discard. Put all ingredients into a cast-iron pan (or other metal pot). Bring to a boil and simmer 20 minutes, covered. Stir occasionally, using a wooden spoon to avoid breaking skin. Baste without cover for 15 minutes more or until half of the liquid remains.

Spoon liquid on wings: Stir frequently for darker, even color.

Note 1: Should be cooked at least 35 minutes. If your liquid evaporates too soon, you may have to add just a little liquid to keep wings from getting too salty.

Note 2: When chicken starts to fall off of the bone, it should be done. If using de-boned chicken, when pierced with a fork and it falls apart, it should be done.

Serve with or on rice. (Optional)

SWEET & SOUR CHICKEN STIR FRY

(Gluten-Free Version by Adrienne Z. Milligan
from a recipe on the Smucker's® website)

½ cup SMUCKER'S® Low Sugar Apricot Preserves
1 tablespoon vinegar
1 teaspoon garlic salt
1 teaspoon ginger
1 teaspoon GF soy sauce
⅛ teaspoon crushed red pepper flakes
2 medium zucchini

2 whole large chicken breasts—skinned, boned and cut into 1-inch cubes
¼ cup oil
½ pound small mushrooms, sliced
½ teaspoon salt
1—6-ounce package frozen pea pods, thawed
Hot cooked rice, if desired

Combine apricot preserves, vinegar, garlic salt, ginger, soy sauce and crushed red pepper flakes; stir until well blended. Set aside.

Halve zucchini lengthwise. Cut into ¼-inch slices; set aside. Heat 2 Tablespoons oil in wok (or Dutch oven) over high heat; stir-fry chicken until tender and browned.

Add remaining oil, zucchini, mushrooms and salt to chicken. Stir-fry until zucchini is crisp-tender. Add pea pods and apricot sauce; toss gently to mix well and heat through.

Serve with hot cooked rice (if desired). Yield: 4 servings.

ADRIENNE'S ROAST AND GRAVY

[Note: The following needs be prepared according to personal taste and the number of people being served, as regards amounts and poundage of the meat.]

Place a frozen roast [a thawed or fresh roast will obviously take less time] fat side down into a crock-pot. Add fresh basil, fresh oregano, fresh parsley, freshly ground pepper, dash of kosher sea salt, and minced garlic. Add chopped onions, carrots, celery, and potatoes. If pieces are too big, they won't cook completely. If the pieces are too small, they'll be mush long before the roast is done.

Pour in one or two cans of cola soda (with or without caffeine, doesn't have to be name brand)—but do NOT use diet (it won't cook right due to artificial sweeteners). Add water to fill up rest of crock pot, leaving a good inch or two for liquid to rise as the roast thaws.

Cover and put on low. Cook on low for about 10-12 hours or until roast falls apart when pricked with a fork.

We like putting on the roast around midnight (to have roast for lunch), or putting it on about 5-6 A.M. for a 5-6 P.M. dinner.

AFTER you remove the roast to a serving platter and the vegetables to a large serving bowl, pour ALL of the drippings from the crock pot into a large pot. Turn on high and bring to a rapid boil.

Using a whisk, slowly add in 1 teaspoon of xanthan gum and stir until completely mixed in. Let this boil for a couple of minutes and then test thickness by ladling some out. If too thin, add in another teaspoon of xanthan gum and then repeat. Remember that the gravy will thicken as it cools. Unless very thick gravy is desired, or you're cooking for a very large crowd, 3 teaspoons of xanthan is usually the maximum amount you'll ever need use.

FOR A MEATLESS GRAVY: The authors know many who do not eat meat. We like to make meatless gravy by using Imagine's® No-Chicken Chicken Broth (all vegetables, no meat products whatsoever) and follow the same directions for the above gravy. No one can tell the difference between this gravy and others.

Note: Gravy CAN be made with cornstarch mixed with water. It can also be made with white-rice flour. Try a couple of different starches/flours and see what you like best. If you prefer lumps in your gravy, xanthan gum may not be what you will want to use, as it makes pretty smooth gravy.

ADRIENNE'S MEATLOAF

1 pound ground beef
½ pound sausage
½ large onion, chopped
½ cup mushrooms, chopped (optional)
1 egg
¼ to ½ cup cornmeal (fat content of meat, humidity in air, as well as consistency of meat mixture will all go into determining how much cornmeal you use; this is usually a trial and error learning process that you'll eventually master through practice)
minced garlic
ground black pepper
fresh basil, oregano, parsley—to taste
spaghetti sauce (8 ounces)
cheese (can be string cheese or cheese that's been cubed)
2 Tablespoons brown sugar

Preheat oven to 350 F. In large bowl, combine ground beef, sausage, onion, mushrooms, egg, cornmeal, seasonings, including brown sugar, and spaghetti sauce. In a large bread pan, put in half of meat mixture. Make an indentation in the center lengthwise of entire loaf. Add cheese to the indentation. Put rest of meat mixture on top and then shape entire loaf. Bake 45 to 50 minutes or until meat is done.

Drain off excess grease (very carefully) by using large spatula or other utensil to hold loaf in pan with one hand while using other hand (with oven mitt on) to hold and tip the pan.

Variation: Place loaf onto baking rack that is sitting on top of a cookie sheet or jelly-roll pan to catch any grease dripping. If using a flat, no-sided cookie sheet, foil should be folded up along all of its sides to construct a catching mold—otherwise grease can run off the flat surface, especially when you remove the finished results from the oven.

ADRIENNE'S DUTCH OVEN MEATLOAF

("Tweaking" courtesy of N7NAP and Diane)

4 pounds of ground beef (or you can use ground beef and sausage)
3 large onions, chopped
½ cup to 1½ cups of cornmeal (fat content of meat, humidity in air, as well as consistency of meat mixture will all go into determining how much cornmeal you use; this is usually a trial and error learning process that you'll eventually master through practice)
2 eggs
1—25-ounce (or thereabouts) jar of spaghetti sauce

- 2 leaves each of fresh basil, oregano, thyme, and parsley (or to taste)
- 20 turns of black pepper mill (or to taste)
- 2 heaping Tablespoons of minced garlic (or to taste)
- 3 Tablespoons brown sugar
- grated cheddar cheese (or can use pepper jack, Colby jack, or a combination thereof)
- ketchup—for on top of meatloaf
- carrots and red potatoes—cut up and steamed on high in microwave for 5-10 minutes (to be added later)

This recipe is designed for an 8-quart-deep Camp Dutch oven 12-inch in diameter. You can line the oven with foil if desired, but it's not necessary if it is only used for GF cooking. If the oven has been used for gluten-containing food, then lining IS necessary to avoid cross-contamination.

Preheat charcoal and prepare enough for a 14-inch Dutch oven (NOTE: *there needs to be enough charcoal already hot and ready to use in case you need to add more heat for the meatloaf*). When placing charcoal on oven, use 12-14 on top and 10 on bottom. (If baked in the oven, the temperature would be at 350 F.) Make sure to arrange the coals so that they are spread out to cover as much surface area as possible.

Combine meat with onions, cornmeal, eggs, spaghetti sauce, herbs, ground pepper, garlic, and brown sugar. Mix in cheese. Take the mixture and form a ring inside the Dutch oven. Make sure that the ring is touching the Dutch oven to allow it to cook completely.

After about 30 minutes, add the pre-micro-waved carrots and red potatoes to center of ring. Add more coals as needed. When there is 15 minutes left, spoon/spread ketchup onto top of ring. Use a meat thermometer to make sure ring is done. When cooked in the oven at 350 F., my meatloaf with 1.5 pounds of meat takes anywhere from 45-60 minutes to be completely cooked. Please take this into consideration when preparing this in the Dutch oven with 4 pounds of meat.

▶ *Potatoes*

SCALLOPED POTATOES

(Gluten-Free Version by Adrienne Z. Milligan from *Wheat-Free Recipes and Menus: Delicious Dining Without Wheat or Gluten*, by Carol Fenster, Ph.D.)

Preheat oven to 350 F.

Toss the following in a 1½-quart casserole or baking dish:

4 medium russet potatoes (peeled, sliced)
¾ tsp Gluten-Free onion salt
¼ tsp white pepper
1 Tbsp Gluten-Free onion flakes

Combine the following in a jar with a screw top lid:

⅛ tsp ground nutmeg
½ tsp dried mustard
1 Tbsp cooking oil
2 Tbsp potato starch or sweet rice flour
2 cups skim or 1% milk (or rice or soy milk)

1 Tbsp parmesan cheese (cow, rice, or soy—optional)

Shake thoroughly until ingredients are blended. Or, blend in blender until smooth. Pour milk mixture over potatoes. Dot with butter cubes (1 Tbsp butter or margarine, in ¼ inch cubes). Lightly sprinkle with paprika.

Bake for 1 hour or until sauce is bubbly and potatoes are lightly browned.

SCALLOPED POTATOES WITH HAM: Add 1 cup cubed ham and reduce onion salt to ½ tsp.

Serves 4.

▶ *Soup*

OLIVE'S HAMBURGER SOUP

(Gluten-Free Version by Adrienne Z. Milligan and William Maltese)

2 Tablespoons butter
1 chopped onion
1 Tablespoon minced garlic (or to taste)
1 pound ground beef
1 cup chopped celery with leaves
1 cup diced carrots
1 7-ounce can whole kernel corn, undrained
1 7-ounce can of diced tomatoes, undrained
¼ cup Gluten-Free elbow macaroni
½ teaspoon pepper
2 teaspoons salt
2 cups diced potatoes
2 Gluten-Free beef bouillon cubes (if desired)
2½ quarts of hot water

In large kettle or stock pot, cook onion in butter until tender. Add beef and minced garlic. Cook, stirring until beef is crumbly. Add hot water, bouillon cubes (if desired), veggies, salt, pepper, and macaroni. Bring to a boil.

Cover and simmer until veggies are tender (approximately 1½ hours). Taste and adjust seasoning as desired.

Serves 8.

► *Pasta Salad*

Zabby's Pasta Salad

1 pound ground beef
1 large onion, chopped
1 package of Trader Joe's® or Tinkyada's® Brown-Rice Penne
1 large can of diced tomatoes (can be seasoned or not)
oregano, parsley, basil, rosemary, thyme, freshly ground black pepper (to taste)
cheese, if desired

Cook ground beef and onion with seasonings. Drain. Cook pasta according to package directions. Drain and put back into pot. Stir in meat mixture and diced tomatoes. Heat up to serve warm, or salad may be served cold.

Grate cheese over entire pot (or bowl if serving cold), or let each person grate their own.

Variation: Cube cheese and stir into salad; can also add cubed cucumbers, olives, and so on. For a twist, use GF pasta spirals.

▶ *Pancakes*

BUTTERMILK PANCAKES

(Gluten-Free Version by Adrienne Z. Milligan from *Better Homes and Gardens New Cookbook*'s Buttermilk Pancakes)

¼ cup tapioca starch
¼ cup rice bran
¼ cup millet flour
¼ cup coconut flour
1 Tablespoon sugar
1 teaspoon baking powder
½ teaspoon baking soda
¼ teaspoon salt
1 beaten egg (bring to room temperature first, then beat separately)
1 cup buttermilk
2 Tablespoons cooking oil

Stir together flours, sugar, baking powder, baking soda, and salt. In separate bowl, beat egg. Add beaten egg and cooking oil to buttermilk. Stir and let stand 5 minutes.

Add milk mixture to flour mixture all at once. Stir just until blended but still slightly lumpy. Don't over-stir. Pour about ¼ cup batter onto hot and lightly greased griddle or heavy skillet for a standard size pancake. Use about 1 Tablespoon of batter for a dollar-size pancake.

Cook until pancake is golden brown (lift it's edge with pancake flipper to check); turn pancake over to cook its second side when upper surface is bubbly and has slightly dry edges.

Makes 8 to 10 standard size pancakes or 36 dollar-size pancakes.

▶ Breads and Pie Dough

A Note from the Authors:

As mentioned earlier in the book, make a recipe once as written. Keep a record of what you like and don't like about the finished product. Make the recipe again, keeping in mind what you liked and disliked, and attempt to revise the recipe to eliminate your dislikes. I've changed the flours in the bread-flour mix to suit our tastes and to counteract how members of my family sometime react to certain flours even if GF.

The following are Adrienne's tweaked versions of some yummy recipes. Feel free to swap out the flours as you see fit—just remember that certain flours work better (or not) in breads versus desserts. One of the best ways to learn about the different flours is to try them out in different recipes and ratios and see what does and doesn't work for you and for your taste buds.

Tip from the Fearless Bread Chef, Reginald Beck, on Measuring Flours:

When you're measuring flour, don't just scoop the measuring cup into the bag or container. Use a large scoop or mixing spoon and gently shake flour into the measuring cup until it heaps. Then, level it off with a knife or other straight edged utensil. This will prevent the flour from compacting and prevent you from adding too much flour to the recipe.

ALL-PURPOSE FLOUR MIX

(From a recipe handed out at GF-Baking Class taught by the Fearless Bread Chef, Reginald Beck)

brown-rice flour	2 parts	2 cups	6 cups
potato starch	⅔ parts	⅔ cups	2 cups
tapioca starch	⅓ part	⅓ cup	1 cup
Total Mix:		3 cups	9 cups

Note: Adrienne uses brown-rice flour and tapioca starch as her main flour mix (equal parts). Sometimes she uses equal parts of white-rice flour and tapioca starch. Other times it is equal parts of brown-rice flour, white-rice flour, and tapioca starch. Often white-rice flour, rice bran, corn flour, cornstarch, coconut flour, millet flour and others are used depending upon the recipe. Adrienne is constantly tweaking flours in each recipe to get just the right taste and texture that her family enjoys the most. Therefore, try a recipe and then tweak it yourself if you choose to do so.

BREAD FLOUR MIX

(Gluten-Free version from a recipe handed out at GF-Baking Class taught by the Fearless Bread Chef, Reginald Beck)

¼ part millet flour	½ cup	1½ cups
¼ part coconut flour	½ cup	1½ cups
1/6 part cornstarch	⅓ cup	1 cup
1/6 part potato starch	⅓ cup	1 cup
1/6 part tapioca starch	⅓ cup	1 cup
Total Mix:	2 cups	6 cups

Note: Due to the millet and coconut flours, keep the bread-flour mix (as well as the millet and coconut flours, if also kept separately) in the refrigerator in air-tight containers. The high oil content in millet, coconut, and other flours will go rancid fast if not kept refrigerated.

SANDWICH BREAD

(Gluten-Free version from a recipe handed out at GF-Baking Class taught by the Fearless Bread Chef, Reginald Beck)

Bring all ingredients to room temperature (this is important):

2 eggs plus 1 yolk
3 Tablespoons canola oil
2 cups bread flour mix

1½ teaspoon xanthan gum
¼ teaspoon salt
2 heaping Tablespoons sugar
¼ ounce (1 pack—check for weight) of active dry yeast
¾ cup plus 2 Tablespoon of buttermilk, heated to 110 F. degrees (can use milk—cow, rice, almond, soy—equal exchange)

Place rack in center of oven and preheat to 375 F. (use gas or electric oven; convection oven will brown the bread too quickly). Grease an 8½ x 4½-inch bread pan and set aside. Mix oil and eggs together and set aside.

Add all dry ingredients to a large mixer bowl and whisk together. Add egg mixture to dry and toss slightly. Add warm milk and mix till just combined.

Scrape bowl and beaters, beat on high for 3 minutes, and then scrape bowl and beaters again. (This *can* be mixed together using an electric hand mixer!)

Dough will be wet and sticky. Use a spatula to transfer to prepared pan and then level dough. Cover with a piece of plastic wrap that has had been oiled (spray with non-stick GF spray or use a pastry brush and brush on shortening). Let rise in a warm and draft-free place for 30-40 minutes or until dough rises to just below the top of the bread pan. Gently remove the plastic wrap, place risen loaf in oven, and *turn heat down to 350 F.*

Bake for 10 minutes and then cover loaf loosely with a foil tent. Bake an additional 20-25 minutes till done.

Remove from pan by running knife along edges then inverting onto cooling rack. Bread will have hollow sound if done when tapped on the bottom. Turn loaf upright, and brush its top crust with butter or margarine while still hot. Let cool 20 minutes before slicing.

Tip: Use active dry yeast instead of rapid-rise or instant yeast. The Gluten-Free yeast bread dough needs to rise slowly (30 minutes minimum) to allow the xanthan gum to set.

BREADSTICKS

(Gluten-Free version from a recipe handed out at GF-Baking Class taught by the Fearless Bread Chef, Reginald Beck)

Make a batch of Gluten-Free Sandwich Bread (See recipe included in this book), but instead of greasing bread pan, grease jelly-roll pan or cookie sheets.

To make the breadsticks, spoon bread dough into a large Zip-Loc® bag that has been sprayed or brushed with GF oil or shortening. Seal and then cut off one bottom corner. Squeeze bag (just like when decorating a cake) and make the breadsticks on the pan. Let rise for same amount of time as bread.

Bake for 15 minutes or until golden brown. (First pan will usually let you know how long to do the remaining pans). Brush breadsticks with butter while still hot. If desired, grate parmesan over them.

Serve and enjoy!

TRADITIONAL PIE CRUST

(Gluten-Free version from a recipe handed out at GF-Baking Class taught by the Fearless Bread Chef, Reginald Beck)

1 cup plus 2 Tablespoon Gluten-Free all purpose flour mix
2 Tablespoon white-rice flour
1 Tablespoon granulated white sugar (omit if using for a savory pie filling)
½ teaspoon xanthan gum
¼ teaspoon salt
6 Tablespoon cold (not room temperature) butter (not margarine), cut in 6 pieces
1 large egg
2 teaspoon cold orange juice or lemon juice

Spray 9-inch pie pan or tart pan (with removable bottom) with GF cooking spray. Then dust the pan with the white-rice flour. Mix flour, sugar, xanthan gum, and salt in large bowl of electric mixer. Add butter (one piece at a time) and mix until crumbly and resembling coarse meal. Add egg and orange juice. Mix on low speed until dough holds together, it should not be sticky.

Form dough into ball, using your hands, and place on a sheet of wax paper. Top with a second sheet of wax paper and flatten dough to 1-inch thickness. (Dough can be frozen at this point for up to one month—wrap in plastic wrap and then use foil as an outer wrap before placing in freezer.)

Roll out dough between the 2 sheets of wax paper. If dough seems tacky, refrigerate for 15 minutes before proceeding. Remove top sheet of wax paper and invert dough into pie pan. Remove remaining sheet of wax paper. Crimp edges for single-crust pie. (Dough can be frozen at this point for up to one month—wrap in plastic wrap and then use foil as an outer wrap before placing in freezer.)

To prebake a bottom pie crust: Preheat oven to 375 F. Gently prick pastry in 3 or 4 places with a fork. Bake pastry for about 25 minutes or until golden brown. Remove from oven and cool completely on a wire rack.

Prebake pie shells can be stored in airtight containers or plastic wrap in refrigerator for 3 days. For longer storage, wrap in plastic wrap and then in foil to store in freezer for up to 2 weeks.

To partially bake a bottom crust: Preheat oven to 375 F. Bake pastry for 10 minutes. Remove from oven. Fill and bake as per recipe.

JENNIFER BURWOOD'S PIE CRUST

a scant cup of brown-rice flour
slightly heaping ½ cup of tapioca starch
slightly heaping ½ cup of potato starch
⅛ teaspoon baking powder
dash of salt
2 Tablespoons of golden flaxseed meal
½ teaspoon xanthan gum

Mix well.

Blend together:

¼ cup unsalted butter (very cold); ¼ cup shortening (very cold). Cut with pastry blender until the size of small peas.
1 egg
1½ teaspoons cider vinegar
3 Tablespoons cold water

Gently combine blended ingredients with flour mixture (add more water if needed). Have filling ready to go before rolling out and/or to have finished as soon as the crust is done. Split dough in half and roll out on floured wax paper. Flour rolling pin. Roll out to ⅛-inch thick.

For bottom crust, lightly flour top of crust and roll onto rolling pin to move to pie tin. Fill in the crust with filling.

For top crust, same as bottom crust, as long as dough doesn't sit for any length of time. If dough sits, it becomes a two-person job to flip the crust (with each person holding two corners of the wax paper) onto the top of the pie.

Bake according to filling directions. Place foil or crust protector around crust, as it tends to brown fast. Remove the crust protector 10-15 minutes before pie is finished cooking.

Makes Two Crusts.

APPENDICES

NOTE

Please be advised that the information in the Appendices that follow is current only as to the time the book was written. Changes should be expected to have occurred since then.

APPENDIX A

CELIAC DISEASE SUPPORT GROUPS

Celiac Disease Foundation®—Lists research and other important information.
> http://www.celiac.org/

Celiac Sprue Association®—Important for research and medical findings.
> http://www.csaceliacs.org/index.php

Gluten Intolerance Group of North America®—Lists chapters/support group information.
> http://www.gluten.net/

Google® Groups—Search for same key words as discussed throughout this book to find groups already started. Start your own group! Whether with GIG®, Yahoo® Groups, Google® Groups, or Meetup.com®, if you find people that want to get support and more information, get your own group going.
> http://groups.google.com

Meetup.com®—Do a search for Celiac Disease, Celiac Sprue, Gluten-Intolerant to see if there are support groups near you.

http://www.meetup.com/

APPENDIX B

GF-Dedicated Companies That Make/Carry Only GF Products

Against The Grain®—Store in Salt Lake City area that carries a large variety of Gluten-Free products from numerous companies.
http://www.againstthegrainslc.com

Cream Hill Estates®—Guaranteed GF oats and oat products.
http://creamhillestates.com

DADs® Gluten-Free Pizza Crust.
http://www.glutenfreepizza.com

Desert Essence Organics®—Awesome and safe bath products.
http://www.desertessence.com/solutions

Chebe® Bread Products—Good bread products that are really yummy.
http://www.chebe.com/

flying apron bakery®.
http://www.flyingapron.net

Gluten-Free Oats®.
http://www.glutenfreeoats.com

Gluten-Free Savonnerie®—They have great soap that's not only Gluten-Free, but artificial-coloring free and fragrance free as well.
http://gfsoap.com/

Glutino® & Gluten-Free Pantry®—We love the Glutino® Pretzels and order them by the case!
http://www.glutino.com

Haley's Corner Bakery®—This is a bakery in Kent, Washington, that bakes 100% GF. It has a fabulous angel food cake! They also do take-'n'-bake pizzas, breads, pies, cakes, cookies, and more.
http://www.haleyscorner.com

Kinnikinnick Foods, Inc.®—Check local frozen food section of natural food market and/or grocery store for their frozen breads, donuts, and more.
http://consumer.kinnikinnick.com

1-2-3 Gluten-Free, Inc. ®—Makes mixes for cakes, cookies, brownies, rolls, and breads.
http://123glutenfree.com

Sunny Valley Wheat Free®—This is the bakery in Maple Valley, Washington, that has the BEST Maple Bars EVER! She also makes breads, cookies, bars, homemade pasta (egg noodles!), and more.
http://www.sunnyvalleywheatfree.com

Sweet Beauty Organic Chocolate Spa® Treatments—We (the authors) love their Taste Lip Balm.
http://www.sweetbeautyspa.com/default.aspx

The Cravings Place®—Makes mixes sold in Fred Meyer®, natural food markets, and elsewhere.
http://www.thecravingsplace.com

Tinkyada® Rice Pasta—We use Tinkyada's rice lasagna noodles for Jonathan's lasagna and no one can tell we haven't used a gluten-saturated product.
http://www.tinkyada.com

APPENDIX C

COMPANIES THAT MAKE GF PRODUCTS

Amy's Kitchen®.
http://www.amyskitchen.com

Annie's Homegrown®.
http://www.annies.com

Bakery On Main®.
http://bakeryonmain.com/wheat_gluten_free.html

Betty Crocker®—Betty Crocker® has four new GF dessert mixes on store shelves nationwide: Chocolate Brownie Mix, Chocolate Chip Cookie Mix, Devil's Food Cake Mix, and Yellow Cake Mix.
http://www.bettycrocker.com/products/gluten-free/gluten-free.htm

Blue Diamond Growers®.
http://www.bluediamond.com

Bob's Red Mill®—This was the first company from which I ordered GF flours. It's still my number-one choice, as I know that their milling practices are 100% GF (for their GF products are all produced and packaged in a separate facility).
>http://www.bobsredmill.com

Butterball®—Butterball® labels their turkeys that are GF!
>http://www.butterball.com

Corazonas® Heart-Healthy Snacks.
>http://corazonas.com

DeBoles® Gluten-Free Pasta—They have rice pasta. Check package label for GF status.
>http://www.deboles.com/products/Gluten-Free-products.php

Ener-G Foods®.
>http://www.ener-g.com

French Meadow Bakery®.
>http://www.frenchmeadow.com/products/vmchk/Gluten-Free

General Mills® Chex Cereals®— BE SURE to CHECK LABELS for GF status. Rice Chex®, Corn Chex®, Honey Nut Chex®, Chocolate Chex®, Cinnamon Chex®, and Strawberry Chex® now come GF! However, check labels, as older boxes will be sold first (and older boxes have gluten in them).

http://www.chex.com/Recipes/GlutenFree.aspx

Imagine®—Has pseudo-chicken broth (but smells just like the real thing), super yummy tomato soup, mushroom soup, squash soup and much more! All natural, no fillers, and most are Gluten-Free (check site and packaging to be sure). Beware—Imagine® products are made with REAL ingredients so the flavors are natural and strong (but, oh so good!).
http://www.imaginefoods.com/info/faq.php#allergens

La Tortilla Factory® Gluten-Free Wraps
http://www.latortillafactory.com

McCann's® Irish Oatmeal.
http://www.mccanns.ie/p_QuickCook.html

Nature's Path®—Lots of good cereals, cereal bars, and waffles.
http://www.naturespath.com

Notta® Pasta.
http://www.nottapasta.com

Pamela's Products®—Six flavors of Gluten-Free Waffles and Gluten-Free Cinnamon French Toast. Yummy. We have found them best if toasted twice.
http://www.pamelasproducts.com

Thai Kitchen®—We love making Pad Thai and use Thai Kitchen's Pad Thai Sauce.

http://www.thaikitchen.com

thinkThin® Protein Bars.
http://shop.thinkproducts.com/thinkproducts.aspx?ProductLine=1002

Trader Joe's®—They have a lot of GF products—both by other companies as well as under their own label (waffles, pastas and more). Trader Joe's® Rice Pasta and Cheddar Cheese is THE BEST Mac & Cheese out there (Gluten-Free or otherwise) in our opinion. They also don't add artificial food coloring to their cheese sauce (like one unmentioned major name-brand does).
http://www.traderjoes.com

Valley Fresh® 100% Natural Premium White Chicken.
http://www.valleyfresh.com/healthyliving/glutenfree.aspx

Van's All Natural Foods® Gluten-Free.
http://www.vansfoods.com/home/Gluten-Free

Whole Foods Markets®—They carry many GF products by other companies. The cool thing about Whole Foods® is that they built a 100% GF baking facility and now carry their own frozen GF foods—breads, desserts, and more.
http://www.wholefoodsmarket.com

APPENDIX D

STORES THAT CARRY GF PRODUCTS

flying apron bakery®—Some genuinely delicious desserts.
http://www.flyingapron.net/home.htm

Fred Meyer®—Look in the natural foods section—be sure to check out frozen section, too.
http://www.fredmeyer.com/Pages/default.aspx

G.F. Joe's® Market—This is the ultimate in GF shopping in our area! G.F. Joe's carries over 1,300 GF products—pasta, frozen food, chips, cookies, and a lot more—name brands and local brands.
http://www.gfjoes.com

Hmart®—Lots of GF foods, here—be sure to read labels or ask (not all labels are in English).
http://www.hmart.com/index.asp

IGA®—We love going to IGA® for GF foods, especially when vacationing in Canada!
http://www.iga.com/consumer/default.aspx

Marlene's Market & Deli Natural Foods®—Marlene's carries a lot of GF foods as well as other GF items like bath products, hand soaps, and more.
http://www.marlenesmarket-deli.com/

PCC Natural Markets®.
http://www.pccnaturalmarkets.com/

Pilgrim's Market®.
http://www.pilgrimsmarket.com/

QFC®.
http://www.qfc.com/Pages/default.aspx

Safeway®.
http://www.safeway.com/IFL/Grocery/Home

Trader Joe's®.
http://www.traderjoes.com/index.html

Wal-Mart®—The Wal-Mart® store brand usually lists GF status. They have made a big effort for accuracy in this area.
http://www.walmart.com/

Whole Foods Markets®.
http://www.wholefoodsmarket.com/

APPENDIX E

RESTAURANTS WITH GF MENUS (OR, AT THE LEAST, GF FRIENDLY)

Biaggi's Italian Restaurants®—We are waiting for Biaggi's to open a restaurant closer to us (down the street would be awesome). Until then, we dine at Biaggi's every time we pass through Salt Lake City, Utah. They have a GF menu on their website as well as in house. This is one of three family favorites for us!
http://www.biaggis.com

Claim Jumper Restaurants®—Look under Menu tabs, then Dietary Concerns, and then click on Gluten-Free menu.
http://www.claimjumper.com/hypertext/home.htm

Clarie's Corner Copia®.
http://www.clairescornercopia.com/index.html

Cold Stone Creamery®—Be sure to ask that the staff clean the slab and use clean utensils when they make your ice cream. Check out their website for a list of products that are GF.

http://www.coldstonecreamery.com/nutritional/nutrition_ingredients.html

Corina Bakery & Bistro®—Good GF Cheesecake. Call ahead to make sure they still have GF items left or place an order.
http://corinabakery.com

Garlic Jim's Famous Gourmet Pizza®—Check with your local Garlic Jim's to see if they carry the GF crust.
http://www.garlicjims.com

Golden Spoon® Frozen Yogurt®—Really yummy!!!
http://www.goldenspoon.com

Hemingway's Restaurant®.
http://www.hemingwaysrestaurant.com

Outback Steakhouse®—Has GF menu on website as well as in house. We enjoy their "Chocolate Thunder from Down Under."
http://www.outback.com/

Picazzo's® Gourmet Pizza, Salad, & Pasta—We had Picazzo's® GF Pizza in January 2006. It was the first time my boys had eaten GF pizza "out."
http://www.picazzos.com

Pizza Works®.
http://pizzawrks.com

The Old Spaghetti Factory®—Has GF menu on their website as well as in house. Be sure to anticipate a little bit of extra time as they have to cook the pasta once it is ordered.
http://www.osf.com/menu/Gluten-Free-menu.html

13 Coins Restaurant®—Let your server know about your food sensitivities and/or allergies, and he or she will do all he or she can to accommodate. This is one of three family favorites for us!
http://www.13coins.com

Uno Chicago Grill®—They just added GF pizza to their regular menu at most locations. They have a GF menu on their website.
http://www.unos.com/index.html

Woody's on the Water®—The atmosphere is quaint, and the view is awesome. One of the owner's daughters has CD/is GF and they are aware of GF dietary needs. This is one of three family favorites for us!
http://www.woodystacoma.com

Z'Tejas Southwestern Grill®—Has GF menu on website and in-house. As of writing this book, we have eaten here twice. Good food.
http://www.ztejas.com

APPENDIX F

OTHER GF WEBSITES

BeFreeForMe®—Coupons for GF products—sign up to receive coupons via email and/or snail mail.
http://www.befreeforme.com

Bob and Ruth's Gluten-Free Dining and Travel Club®—This is on my top ten list of what I want to do! Imagine a vacation where food is NOT something you have to worry about—whether on a cruise ship or a foreign country.
http://bobandruths.com

The Food Allergy and Anaphylaxis Network (FANN) ®—Sign up on this site to receive free email alerts when product recalls are issued by companies for undeclared wheat, gluten, dairy, seafood, nuts, or more.
http://foodallergy.org

INDEX TO GLUTEN-FREE RECIPES

DESSERTS

Flourless Chocolate Torte 99
Bonnie's Xoçai™ XoBiotic™ Chocolate and
   Strawberries Zabaglione 101
Bonnie's Xoçai™ XoBiotic™ Chocolate Tiramisu 102
Bonnie's Xoçai™ XoBiotic™ Chocolate S'mores 104
Bonnie's Xoçai™ XoBiotic™ Chocolate Flourless
   Molten Cake 105
Debra Kaiser's Breakfast Cake 106
Banana Nut Muffins 106
Olive's Big Pan Brownies 108
Byron's Oatmeal Cookies 108
Victor's Peanut Butter Cookies 110
Chocolate Drop Fudge Cookies, No Bake 110
Jell-O® Cookies 111
Grandma Pease's Cookies 112
Lemon Dream Bars 113
Pumpkin Bars 114

CHEESE

Cheese Wafers 116
Zabby's Grilled Cheese Sandwich 117
Lasagna 118
Dave's Tuna Mac & Cheese 120
Elaine's Cheese/Tuna Melts 120
Vikki's Cheese Goulash 121
Cheese- and Asparagus-Stuffed Chicken Breasts 122

MEAT

Corn Dogs 123
Shanghai Chicken Wings 124
Sweet & Sour Chicken Stir Fry 125
Adrienne's Roast and Gravy 126
Adrienne's Meatloaf 128
Adrienne's Dutch Oven Meatloaf 129

POTATOES

Scalloped Potatoes 132

SOUP

Olive's Hamburger Soup 134

PASTA SALAD

Zabby's Pasta Salad 136

PANCAKES

Buttermilk Pancakes 137

BREADS AND PIE DOUGHS

A Note from the Authors 139
Tip on Measuring Flours from Fearless Bread Chef 140
All Purpose Flour Mix 140
Note 140
Bread Flour Mix 141
Note 141
Sandwich Bread 141
Breadsticks 143
Traditional Pie Crust 144
Jennifer Burwood's Pie Crust 145

ABOUT THE AUTHORS

ADRIENNE Z. MILLIGAN was born and continues to live in the Pacific Northwest. She received a B.A. in Liberal Studies (with a dual concentration in U.S. and International Studies at the University of Washington. She and her husband, Jonathan, and their two sons, Kelly and Ozias, have lived the Gluten-Free Way since June 2001, and Adrienne still enjoys finding new treats and products for her and her family, as well as converting gluten recipes into Gluten-Free versions. For more information on Adrienne and the Gluten-Free way, check out her websites:

http://www.theglutenfreewaymyway.com

and

http://mygf-life.blogspot.com

WILLIAM MALTESE was born in the Pacific Northwest, has a B.A. in Marketing / Advertising, and spent an honorable tour of duty in the U.S. Army where he achieved the rank of E-5. He started his career writing for men's pulp magazines, and has since had published more than 200 books, fiction and nonfiction, in every genre, while being honored with his listing in the prestigious *Who's Who in America*. For more information on William, check out his websites:

http://www.theglutenfreewaymyway.com

http://www.williammaltese.com

http://www.myspace.com/williammaltese

http://www.myspace.com/draqual

http://www.myspace.com/maltesecandlegallery

http://www.myspace.com/flickerwarriors

William's Xoçai™ chocolate-for-sale site:

http://www.mxi.myvoffice.com/williammaltese

www.ingramcontent.com/pod-product-compliance
Lightning Source LLC
LaVergne TN
LVHW041624070426
835507LV00008B/435